CONVERSATION AS MINISTRY

STORIES AND STRATEGIES FOR CONFIDENT CAREGIVING

Douglas Purnell

THE PILGRIM PRESS   CLEVELAND

REMEMBERING WITH
GRATITUDE THE GRACE
OF MY FATHER, WALLY,
WHO ENGAGED ME IN
SERIOUS CONVERSATION
ABOUT LIFE FOR OVER
FIFTY YEARS.

The Pilgrim Press, 700 Prospect Avenue, Cleveland, Ohio 44115-1100
pilgrimpress.com
Copyright © 2003 Douglas John Purnell

Scripture quotations, unless otherwise noted, are from the New Revised Standard
Version of the Bible, © 1989 by the Division of Christian Education of the
National Council of Churches of Christ in the United States of America and are
used by permission.

Printed in the United States of America on acid-free paper

08   07   06   05   04   03   5   4   3   2   1

Library of Congress Cataloging-in-Publication Data
Purnell, Douglas, 1946–
    Conversation as ministry : stories and strategies for confident caregiving /
    Douglas Purnell.
        p.   cm.
    Includes bibliographical references.
    ISBN 0-8298-1578-3 (pbk. : alk. paper)
    1. Pastoral care.   2. Conversation—Religious aspects—Christianity.   I. Title.

BV4011.3.P87   2003
253'.7—dc22

                                                                    2003061770

C O N T E N T S

FOREWORD

There has always been an internal tussle between adjectives and nouns in defining the work of care from a religious perspective. The traditional German word *seelsorge,* literally meaning soul care, developed in the United States as pastoral care. Recently, pastoral has been replaced by spiritual as a prevailing modifier of care in chaplaincy. The nouns have shifted as well. Counseling was sometimes thought of as an equivalent to care. Pastoral psychotherapy became the metaphor of choice among those who counsel professionally from a religious perspective. Current interest in spirituality has added spiritual direction or guidance to the repertoire of terms for the religious work of care. In this book, Doug Purnell reworks pastoral conversation as the term for the ministry of care.

In 1962, Heije Faber and Ebel van der Schoot introduced the term pastoral conversation into the panoply of metaphors for soul care in *Het Pastorale Gesprek,* translated in 1965 as *The Art of Pastoral Conversation* (New York: Abingdon Press, 1965). The secret of good conversation, they suggested, is a way of listening and responding that attends to both the content that is spoken and the feelings inside and around the words for all persons in the conversation. The content may not necessarily be religious but pastoral conversation is a hopeful consideration of events in everyday life that have ultimate meaning. "In all pastoral conversation," they wrote, "the primary aim of the pastor is to help the other person see his life in God's light" (page 115). Pastoral conversation is what a pastor does on behalf of the church and in response to the church's authority.

Purnell's reworking of the tradition of *seelsorge* as conversation defines pastoral much more expansively. He argues that every Christian person has a duty and capacity to have pastoral conversations. It is a ministry shared by all. A pastoral person is anyone, lay or ordained, who engages with people in an intentional and reflective process that will help them "enter the deep places where God breaks into their lives." What makes a conversation pastoral for Purnell is that people move together to the deeper places in human life and discover the sacred mysteries by intensifying the ordinary. Conversation is pastoral when at least one person is open to seeing God's light in ordinary places and hearing the voice of God in new ways.

There is a timeliness to Purnell's reintroducing conversation as one of the modes of care from a religious perspective. It corresponds to the new focus on religious practice. Conversation, like the mutual consolation of brothers and sisters, is a practice of faith. Using the noun conversation to describe the work of care is also significant because it shifts the focus from the aim of our work (care) to the means by which this work is done (conversation). Pastoral conversation is a reminder to all caregivers that the goal is never as important as the process. Finally, the focus on conversation relates the work of care to what human beings must do to survive and thrive: talk with one another.

Conversation is a vehicle by which a society constructs reality and safeguards a measure of symmetry between objective and subjective views of the world. In a time when truth is regarded as more subjective than objective, conversation gains in significance as a way of maintaining community among individuals holding a multiplicity of perspectives. Who is "at the table" for the conversation becomes a critical factor for determining the inclusivity for a gathering of people. Technique is important but what matters most is how we stay in the conversation. And we keep talking to one another without quick resolution because we know that conversations seldom stand alone. They are incomplete, ongoing, and somehow interwoven with another conversation somewhere else.

In my experience, conversations that inspire or transform are characterized by a quality of immediacy. Direct and spontaneous responses between people in conversation diminish suspicion and strengthen trust. In my knowing of him, Doug Purnell is a wonderfully immediate, authentic, direct, creative, and compassionate man. When you read this book, you will discover this about him too, for he is seldom absent from its pages. Purnell has embodied on the pages of a book what he hopes the reader will enact in every conversation. You will find this book profoundly spiritual but seldom pious. It is fully human, without pretense. It is wise in a practical sort of way, full of surprising insights into the human struggle.

In recent years, I have often used "pastoral conversation" to describe to someone the nature of our work together. It is an open-ended term that might include some work that would look like spiritual direction. At other times, we might do theological reflection about some significant event in his or her life. Or we might focus on some aspect of living in need of confession or reconciliation. Or we might simply talk together with care as the focus. The second reason why I am drawn to the image of conversation is that it keeps our attention on fashioning an authentic bond based on genuine exchange. The integrity of Doug Purnell is palpable in the way he talks about care. That integrity includes a kind of transparency that makes it possible for people to be surprised by experiences of grace through pastoral conversation.

This book is one half of a conversation with a wise friend: you will have to imagine your side. As the reader, you might imagine yourself looking over Purnell's shoulder as he tells you candid story after candid story about his ministry. Because it is written in a very direct and sometimes hortatory way, you may feel admonished from time to time. Be open to a whole range of things, Purnell urges; be grounded in the worshipping love of a Christian community; be intentional so you can think ahead into the conversation; respect the sacredness of that which is shared with you, be open to conversion; and above all else, be authentic. The irony is that we cannot be admonished into authenticity. As a reader, you can expect to experience the power of authenticity not only in what Purnell proposes about a compassionate conversation but also in the way he writes about it.

Those who are beginning to learn the art of pastoral conversation will find a bounty of practical suggestions in *Conversation as Ministry*. Purnell provides a structure for thinking about the "where, when, and who" of a conversation, and suggestions for how to begin and how to end a conversation. He applies his principles to specific pastoral situations like planning a wedding, talking about matters of faith, helping people in a time of conflict, and ministering at the time of birth or at the time of death. His stories often presume the symbolic weight or authority of being a pastor in a community. Though lay caregivers may not have the authority ascribed to clergy, if they follow the wisdom in these pages, they will find the kind of courageous compassion that evokes trust. When people trust us, it will be possible to walk with them into those spaces in their lives where they will find the voice of God emerging in fresh ways.

—*Herbert Anderson*

Herbert Anderson is Emeritus Professor of Pastoral Theology at Catholic Theological Union, Chicago, and Director of Pastoral Care at St. Mark's Episcopal Cathedral in Seattle.

ACKNOWLEDGMENTS

I love to read books and look at paintings and listen to music, yet I have learned most about life from conversations with people about their living. It has been my privilege to be invited into conversations at times of anguished pain and of carefree celebration. All such conversations reflect the presence of God. Engaging in deep conversation that meets the heart of the other is the core of ministry.

Some years ago I was working in a therapeutic community in a Psychiatric Hospital. Sandra Brown, then a professor in Pastoral Theology at Princeton Theological Seminary, was visiting Australia. I invited her to come to the community with me. We spent a rich time in deep conversation with others. As we were driving home Sandra asked, "What happens in your head between what you hear and see and when you respond?" The question has stayed with me. When I began teaching pastoral theology full time I wanted to give students some resources to engage in conversation intentionally and pastorally. Those things together have led to this book.

The book includes many conversations shared in pastoral ministry. It is important for me to acknowledge the people who have shared these conversations. Some have died quite a while ago. I honor their memory by using their names in the stories (Bruce, Mabel, Bess, Edie, Grace, and Myrtle.) In other stories I have changed material and names to protect their identity. This is always done with a little regret. Changing names and identities probably doesn't affect you as reader because there are truths in the stories that are universal. It affects me because I have learned, grown, and been gifted with wisdom through these conversations with these particular persons.

Many people have been conversation partners to me along the way. I value these shared times immensely. Mac Nicoll read, commented on, and encouraged me to continue after reading early drafts of the manuscript. Herbert Anderson has been a friend and conversation partner for many years whose encouragement to bring this work to publication I greatly appreciate. The Council and Faculty of United Theological College in Sydney have been most supportive and helpful in making available time for study leave and reflection. I wrote some of the manuscript while being artist in residence at Andover Newton Theological School and I thank my friends there for stimulation and interest. Ulrike Guthrie has been most helpful as an editor, seeing the possibility in a manuscript that was a pile of words and asking the questions that shaped its transformation into a lively book.

My wife, Heather, is an open and honest conversation partner whose patience and trust enable me to fly. Our children, Kirsty, Kieren, and Jonathan, with their partners Andrew, Jodie, and Amanda are lifelong conversation partners who daily enrich my living. It is to them that I dedicate this book.

Part One

SHAPING CONVERSATION AS MINISTRY

Pastoral Conversation

To share in pastoral conversation is an extraordinary gift. You are invited into the most intimate spaces where people talk about the very nature of their being human. They share their joy and they share their pain. They reach hard-to-find words of genuine faith. If you are alert to it, they bless you with life-shaping wisdom.

Bruce and Mabel

Bruce and Mabel Gostelow were members of the congregation of which I was pastor. I am using their names out of respect for the lives they lived and the wisdom I gained from the conversations with them. Bruce was a quirky character who sang in the choir, counted the money after church, enjoyed a roll-your-own cigarette, and had his own unique way of addressing people. For him, I was "Padre" or, more often, "Reverend Father"—mostly, he would address me as "Father." I grew to learn that Bruce loved cricket. If a test match were in progress he would always greet me with a half serious request: "Prayers for king and country this morning, Father?" Another experience that had profoundly marked Bruce's life was his involvement in the army during the Second World War.

When I visited Bruce and Mabel a couple of times in their home they told me of their family's struggles and the differing paths their children had taken in adulthood. These conversations were to help me in later pastoral conversations, among them when I visited Mabel in hospital when she learned that she had an inoperable cancer. She was thinking through decisions about the course of treatment: "quality of life over against treatment that will extend my life for short periods," as she put it. Like most of us at a time of major crisis, Mabel was re-thinking her life goals.

Next morning Bruce phoned to ask if he could come and see me in my office. When I offered to go to his home, Bruce insisted he come to my office. He didn't mention Mabel, or her prognosis, but instead began to tell me stories, stories that though very interesting seemed far removed from the present crisis situation. They were stories about his time as a nurse in Changi prison camp, a notorious death camp of World War II.

For over an hour and without my saying a word, he told me story after story of what happened in Changi. Bruce and other former POWs spoke rarely about such painful experiences. Something unusual was happening and, while I felt privileged to hear the stories, I wondered, "What is going on here? Why is Bruce telling me all these stories?" I assume that when people speak, whatever they are saying is making sense to them and it is up to me to figure out its relevance to the present crisis. So here was Bruce, who had just learned that his wife would soon die, telling me stories of finding, cooking, and sharing a rotten egg while in a POW camp forty years earlier. Slowly it dawned on me that Bruce was telling me stories about how he had survived the most difficult time of his life. In so doing he was rehearsing how he would survive the death of his partner, friend, and wife. Far from avoiding the reality of his wife's prognosis, Bruce was living it most deeply and touching a store of wisdom that would help him to live through this crisis.

This conversation continued over some months in hospital, at home, in my office, at church, accompanying Mabel's movements between home and hospital, hospital and home, as she inexorably approached death.

During an Easter week visit to Mabel and Bruce in hospital, Mabel reported that five different people had come to visit her from the church. All brought reports of the Palm Sunday service in which, to their delight, children had had an active part. Mabel told me about one of these women, who didn't see herself as religious, and who had confided that she came to church because I, her pastor, seemed to have a gift of giving her nourishment for the week at the same time as also giving sustenance to those who would identify themselves as religious. The fact that Mabel shared this information was her way of giving me something that made us equal participants in conversation. Receiving such "gifts" empowers the giver.

Bruce's response to the Palm Sunday service was a little different. "Three good hymns and one not so good, Father. But I had a lump in my throat that I've only had once before, at young Alexander's funeral. I could not sing the three good and one not so good hymns." I looked at Bruce, and I looked at Mabel, and then I looked back at Bruce and said, "That's not surprising, Bruce. Mabel is going to die, and whether you are conscious of it or not, you and she are also walking the journey with Jesus into Jerusalem." "Yes," he said, while Mabel smiled a knowing and approving smile. "I'm usually stoical, not emotional." "Yes," I responded, "and sometimes these things jump up and grab you when you least expect them."

We talked some more, I prayed with them, and I left. In that prayer with Bruce and Mabel, I consciously held their lives and these deep and difficult questions together before God. I wanted them to know that their lives were named before God, that the interweaving of wrestling and joy are the honest work of faith.

I visited Mabel a couple of times during the week in which she died. On Tuesday, her eyes fixed on me but her lips were silent. I shared the Aaronic blessing with her: "The Lord bless you and keep you; the Lord make his face to shine upon you and be gracious to you; the Lord lift up his countenance upon you, and give you peace" (Num. 6:24–26). Often when I haven't been sure what to pray, this simple blessing has been most appropriate and powerful. Many times I have prayed it under my breath as I left people with whom I have been in deep conversation.

I saw Mabel again on the day before she died. I sat with her and held her hand for ten minutes, during which she mostly slept. She opened her eyes briefly and looked toward me, but showed no recognition. Not knowing whether she was aware of the prayer or not, I had prayed: "God, open your arms and receive Mabel. Give to her that eternal peace which is yours. Bless and strengthen Bruce and their children at this time. Amen." As I left, I said, "Good-bye, Mabel," aware of the finality of my words. Bruce called next day to tell me that Mabel had died in the night. The next part of the ongoing conversation would be to work with Bruce and his children to create an appropriate funeral service, one that allowed them to acknowledge Mabel's life and to say good-bye to their wife and mother, one that would sustain them and the community of which they were a part in the days to come, one that would remind them of the hope of their faith.

I spent two hours with the Gostelow family helping them to talk about Mabel, planning the funeral and thanksgiving services. Bruce had decided that he wanted to have a cremation service on Monday, then leave time to get used to the fact that Mabel had died, and have a service on Friday giving thanks for her life.

Planning the funeral and thanksgiving services with the family was very important, yet it had its tensions. Two of the adult children (both in their forties) had different worldviews. One was a Christian who, influenced by his wife's near-death experience, believed that death is only the door to a better life and thus death is to be celebrated. The other brother held a more rational and pragmatic view that the funeral service is the farewell, the end. He would not have named himself or his worldview as Christian. In conversation with the family it was important to value both views. The sons, their sister, and their father together needed to find appropriate rituals with words, stories, and symbols to acknowledge the life of Mabel; together they needed to find a sustaining way to interpret her death that would enable them to live into their respective futures.

Conversations are always incomplete, ongoing, and somehow interwoven with other experiences. While I was working with the Gostelow family to plan the funeral service for Mabel, I phoned my parents on the other side of the country and they seemed to want to talk about death. My father had had a brain tumor removed and was uncertain about his life. My mother was living with the reality that her husband had changed significantly and she was anxious about the future. My recent intimate involvement in Mabel's dying and her family's concerns made me more attentive and attuned to my parents.

At the very beginning of the service of thanksgiving, Bruce stood at the lectern, clicked his heels together, reflecting something of the military discipline of forty years previous, and made a statement, which included a warm commendation of me as minister: "I have always respected his 'cloth' and in these last months I have come to respect his warmth, caring, and his humanity. I'm doing this now, not because I want to, but because 'the cloth' says it will be good for me." Standing at attention at the lectern he began to tell us beautiful stories of himself and Mabel. The stories set the scene for the service of thanksgiving: How they met in the office while working together, his going off to war, and his return home, of going to Mabel's home and how her mother kissed him; "If you kissed the mother you kissed the daughter too," he explained. In this way he delightfully set the scene for the service of thanksgiving.

When I spoke with Bruce later, I told him how much I had learned about life from him and Mabel. He talked of it as being a mutual learning. And he concluded, "Then we are friends." Yes, we were friends.

Some time later, Bruce came into the office with a letter from Rosemary, who was one of the elders. One day, early in Mabel's illness, I had told Rosemary of Bruce's greeting to me: "We haven't declared the innings closed, yet, Father." This is an allusion to the game of cricket and "the close of the innings," a metaphor for death. Rosemary decided that when Mabel died she would write a note of sympathy to Bruce using a cricketing metaphor. The card read: "The umpires have lifted the bails. For you, Bruce, your teammates need you to bat on." "Lifting the bails" refers to the time at the end of the day of play or the end of the game when the umpires lift the bails from the stumps, signifying the end of play. It, too, became a metaphor for death. Bruce said to me, "I read it to one son and I was okay. I read it to my other son and I was okay. I read it to my daughter and I was overwhelmed with emotion. And do you know why? Rosemary was speaking to me in my language. It moved me deeply that someone would want to speak to me in my language. And I wanted to show it to you." I had some sense that by inference Bruce was saying to me, "You also have spoken with me in my language through this long and difficult journey."

Bruce named an extraordinary truth for him personally and for pastoral conversation generally. People want to be addressed in their own language. Rosemary was alert to that need and did it well. Bruce was moved deeply. To hear people in their own language will value their living and will bring them to new speech.

When first I began in ministry I understood pastoral conversation to involve active listening and being able to reflect back what I heard the other person to be feeling. I didn't have much of an idea what we should be talking about. I had even less understanding of just what to do to mark the conversation as pastoral. In the years since I have become more confident of my role in pastoral conversation. This story of my walk alongside Bruce and Mabel offers a picture of what can happen in pastoral conversation.

2

CONVERSATION AS CARE:
SHARING WHAT IT IS TO BE HUMAN

"Let me see your face, let me hear your voice," says one lover to another in the Song of Solomon. Being so present to others as to see their faces and hear their voices is the very nature of conversation, for when people are seen and heard, they find new and life-shaping speech.

The couple at the adjacent table in the coffee shop was engaged in this kind of conversation, talking together about their common life, their children, their hopes and concerns for their children's adult lives. It wasn't a conversation flowing with rivers of words; there were obvious and thoughtful silences. The shared coffee time seemed to me to be about being together, about trusting the other to raise concerns, about being heard without having to find profound answers, about being willing to sit in silence, about being willing to be present to the other. The couple's conversation showed mutuality, a moving back and forth as one of them expressed a point of view or a feeling and the other heard and then responded in kind.

When two or more people engage each other in meaningful ways, conversation is happening. It can involve a sharing of thought, question, silence, insight, concern, laughter, forgiveness, confusion, celebration, and much more. All of us want to engage in significant conversation about our lives in safe settings and with people we trust. We all want to be heard and valued in our own language. This book encourages and equips ordinary people to be confident as pastoral conversation partners. Such mutual sharing of what it is to be human is how I think of conversation in this book.

The primary concern of "pastoral" conversations is care of persons. In the story of Bruce and Mabel, my primary concern was to care for them. By "care," I mean being present to and engaging the other in ways that value their whole beings, and their living. This will include valuing their history, their identity, their present, their future, their wellness, their illness, their hope, their despair, their relationships, their faithfulness, their doubt, their thinking, their loving, their hurting, their worship, their meaning making, and so on. By "care" I also encompass the traditional pastoral theological functions of healing, sustaining, guiding, reconciling, and nurturing. Each of these emerges or finds form in intentional conversation.

Throughout this book, I understand "pastoral people" to mean anyone formed in the church, whether lay or ordained, who engages in pastoral conversation. The pastoral dimension of the relationship is nurtured through the intentional and reflective engagement of the pastoral person.

And yet, not everyone who engages in pastoral conversation will be able to name what makes it pastoral. Most simply engage in such conversations as a way of loving others. Their conversation is shaped by their participation in the practices of Christian faith: worship, hymn singing, Eucharist, Bible study, prayer, reflection, and so on. One of my friends has had a tough couple of years that has included a painful marriage breakup. When we meet we talk about our lives. He tells me the struggles and difficulties he has had and then clearly asks, "How are you?" He listens with discipline and specifically mentions the things he has heard. In his presence I know I am talking to someone who cares. Graham is an elder of the church. He worships regularly and has a daily meditative ritual that includes reading and reflecting on a passage of the Bible. In his daily work he is an engineer. His willingness to engage and be formed by the practices of his faith shapes his compassion and care, which pervades every conversation in which he engages.

Through this book I want to encourage people like Graham, people like you, to be more intentional and more confident in engaging in conversation. I want you to know how to take the initiative to enter the deep places in which God's voice breaks into our lives. Early in my ministry I was not confident to engage in conversation because I was uncertain about how to discern the voice of God in ordinary things. People would ask me, "Will you pray for me?" Implied in the question, I thought I heard an unspoken claim: "You are closer to God than I am." I would push the request away by saying, "You have just as much access to God as I do; talk to God yourself." The truth is that I was also scared that I didn't know enough of the Bible to have a serious "religious" conversation. Frozen by my insecurity, I failed to notice the important acknowledgment of my spiritual role that came in their request, and the fact that I could listen with attention and care.

Whereas once I fobbed off this acknowledgment of my priestly role, now I am happy to own it and encourage others to do likewise. Such owning is exemplified by this story of Edna, a parishioner.

Edna

Edna was at the stage of life when her grandchildren, who meant so much to her, had their own boyfriends and girlfriends and interests and they did not visit her any more. Living alone in a small apartment, she wondered, "Who needs me?"

At lunch at church one day I noticed that Edna was distressed and asked if I could come and visit her. She readily agreed. When I visited, she told me that she was "on a downer." She was recalling in detail a number of difficult events in her life, beginning when she was fourteen with laying out the body of her mother after she had died. That was more than sixty years ago. She talked about feeling that her care was inadequate. She recounted other distressing events: caring for her sister, the breakdown of her marriage. The conversation moved beyond recalling these events to naming the important questions she was asking herself, questions that were deeply religious: "What is the value of my life?" "For what will people remember me?" "Will anybody come to my funeral?" "Will anybody recognize my life as valuable?"

To identify and name these questions addresses the "downer" of which Edna had spoken. The questions need answers, but the answers won't come quickly, but rather with careful thought and integrity. Merely to say, "Of course you are valuable, of course we will remember you," wouldn't in itself be a helpful response. Helping Edna evaluate her own life and answer her own questions as part of an ongoing conversation would be important. Naming the questions would give Edna some power and control over her life. And so with her help, I learned that pastoral conversation was not about me having all the right Bible verses to placate Edna's—or anyone else's—

anxiety; it was about recognizing the importance of the questions that she was asking. Pastoral conversation would be genuine if in valuing her questions I offered an ongoing opportunity to address these questions. As I learned these things I became more confident to engage people in deep, open pastoral conversation and I became more confident that I could respond to the request "Will you pray for me?"

When caring people engage others deeply in their living, the conversation is pastoral. It is pastoral when they listen to the experience and language of the other. It is pastoral when they listen intently and without judgment. Sometimes the conversation will go where it seems there are no adequate words to express what is felt. Then the conversation will be pastoral when the caring person respects the silences and waits for appropriate images and words to emerge. In these times caring people will find a resonance and reverberation with the stories of faith. In these spaces they will find the voice of God emerging in fresh ways. This is prayer.

In writing this book I have chosen to share stories like this one about Edna from my own experience in pastoral conversation. I have been in pastoral ministry for more than thirty years. During that time I have written a daily journal reflecting on my life and ministry. This book shares something of what I have learned in that time, drawing upon my various roles as pastor, counselor, therapist, educator, artist, husband, father, son, brother, and friend. Generally, I have changed the stories and names to protect the identity of the people with whom I shared the conversations. In the stories of Bruce and Mabel, and Grace, all of whom have died, I have used their real names out of respect for what I learned from them in the conversations. Because I am interested in conversation that is caring, because I want to encourage people who are part of the community of faith to engage deep, open conversation as part of their ministry of care, because I want to encourage people to meet others in their living, therefore in this text I offer my own experience to personalize the text and I tell stories to stimulate new thoughts and new possibilities. I hope that in looking over my shoulder and overhearing conversations that sometimes worked and sometimes didn't, you will find confidence to engage in pastoral conversation with those in your life. It is a book that I hope will help you to reflect with discipline on your practice in order that your pastoral conversation can be more intentional, more focused, and more rewarding.

There is no single correct way to engage in pastoral conversation. Using the resources provided here you will be helped to find your own way to enhance how you function in that conversation. There are many things that pastoral people can do to enable the best quality of conversation to take place, and I will outline a number of them. Don't try to take it all in or do it all at once. Focus on one thing at a time and practice it. Doing so will build your awareness of and skill in the many dimensions of deep, open, reflective, pastoral conversation. At root what ultimately gives shape to all conversation is that you love the people given to your care. Everything else builds on this.

3

WHAT MAKES CONVERSATION PASTORAL?

Pastoral conversation:

> is grounded in the worshipping life of the Christian community,
>
> involves a deep knowledge for and love of the Christian tradition,
>
> is shaped by participation in the practices of Christian faith,
>
> calls for a reflective awareness of self,
>
> demands a disciplined attending to the other,
>
> meets people in the circumstance and experience of their living,
>
> requires an active and formed imagination,
>
> is open to hearing the voice of God in fresh ways,
>
> bravely addresses God with life's hard questions,
>
> is open to conversion,
>
> and offers the possibility of love, mercy, peace, justice, healing, reconciliation, new birth, wholeness, nurture, and sustenance.

Pastoral conversation gives body to the realm of God on earth.

When I was at university, I thought that for a conversation to be pastoral, I had to speak about Jesus in ways that demanded a faith commitment on the part of the other. I thought there could be no change, no hope without this commitment, without the other changing to become like me. Yet I have come to understand that genuine conversation is about the very opposite—that the conversation itself might change me and my worldview. There is a great paradox in this, for when I am willing to change, then the possibility is there for the other to change too.

Grace

Grace asked me to come and visit her in her little efficiency apartment near the church. In the room where she lived every drawer was open, clothes hanging out from them, and on every flat surface was a Buddha—though her faith tradition was Catholic. She came daily to the Senior Citizens Centre at our church and was actively involved in everything. This day she was hurt and angry. She had just learned that her former husband had died. Her children did not let her know that he was ill and dying. "They had no right to keep that information from me," she said, before she began her story.

She had grown up in a Catholic orphanage where the nuns had taught her that "if your husband was unfaithful, you got rid of him." So when her husband was unfaithful, she asked him to leave. At the time Grace had four small children, it was the 1950s, and there were no pensions to support single mothers. Grace said, "If I had my time over again, I'd have forgiven him and we'd have got on with it." All these years later she would like to have been able to say to him, "I forgive you." I had to rethink my own view on what was primary in marriage: genital exclusivity (being faithfully monogamous) or long-term commitment? The conversation was significant not because I persuaded Grace that she should be different, but because I experienced a conversion that significantly reshaped my worldview. A couple of days later I sat quietly beside Grace at her husband's funeral aware of much that wouldn't be spoken out loud.

At a later time I thought that pastoral conversation would involve talking in some meaningful way about God. I rarely seemed able to do that. I didn't seem to have the language and neither did the people I was meeting. I will never forget the day that changed.

Toad Hall

I had been working in a newly established therapeutic community in a psychiatric hospital called Toad Hall. Even though the community tried to forget whether people were doctors or nurses or patients, some got angry with me because I was a chaplain, and as a chaplain I represented God. It got to me. So, one morning I brought a trash can. I drew images of the church and God and pious clergy on it, then took it to the community meeting and said, "I am sick of getting your 'shit' for God and the church. Put it in this bin." And they did! Then I offered to run a special session where people could be angry with God.

If they would express their anger for God, I, as a representative of God, would be there to listen. On that day I brought along paint and large sheets of paper and invited people to express on the paper their anger for God. They did. The images they created and the stories they told left me shaking. Because I had been willing to hear the anger of these people toward God, I was given an entree into hearing their more genuine struggles with life, and therefore with God. The gift to me was that I suddenly found a way to enable people to talk about God in their own language.

If I had imagined that pastoral conversation was the domain of clergy persons, those who'd been specially trained, I quickly realized that every person had a right and capacity to engage in pastoral conversation. It is a ministry shared by all.

I learned that many lay people were reluctant practitioners because they were uncertain about what was expected of them. They didn't know that such uncertainty belonged to clergy and lay people alike. And so, even though I was uncertain about what I was doing, I invited lay people to join me when I was visiting. Afterwards we would reflect together on what had happened in the conversation. Together we developed a confidence to move into conversation.

The people who engage in pastoral conversation are those who genuinely want to meet with and hear about the living of others. Those who enact this care are often formed in the practices of the Christian faith. Pastoral persons are those who respond to Jesus' commandment to love one another. They know, even if they cannot clearly name, that when they engage in this conversation they are somehow enacting God's presence in the world.

In my conversation with Grace, I went to someone I heard hurting. My intention was to be present and listen. I discovered a person, made in God's image, anguishing over questions that I had never imagined. When carers are present to others in their living, when they are willing to be with them, without answers or great wisdom, without trying to change them or make them into something different, they are engaging in pastoral conversation. Such conversation means being present to the other person as someone who, in his or her difference, is a carrier of the divine image. We are all made in God's image and pastoral persons know and value that God is present in every person. They see God in the other and reflect God in their own being.

Visiting after the fires

As I write this, people in Canberra, Australia's national capital, are cleaning up after being ravaged by fires during the night. More than 550 homes have been destroyed. The devastation is vast.

Twenty years ago, with a group of people I walked through an area that had been heavily affected by fire, with the intent of engaging whomever we could in conversation. People were distressed and in shock; they were angry, irrational, and emotional. We hoped that if we could get them to talk we would be helping them move forward just a little bit.

Never in my life have I been more uncertain about what I was doing as I walked among the ruins. Many whose homes had been burned had gone to stay with friends. The ones who remained were coping with the distress of having lived through the fire and the mystery of why one house was burned and the one next door not. Where we could, we engaged people in conversation: "Tell me about your experience." And people did, telling us of how the fires had sucked away their breath. Their breathing was shallow, their words came out falteringly, their eyes were red and darting. Such tough stories. Such hurting people.

At the end of the day I was uncertain as to what I had achieved by being there. A young man stopped his truck at a hydrant and filled it with water. I tried to engage him in conversation. He was task focused. I said something inane like, "It is alright for you; you know what you are doing. You are carrying water." He wasn't at all interested in my uncertainty, and simply said, "We all have our job to do." Then he climbed in his truck and drove away. Being in conversation often has this element of helplessness where the only resource you have is yourself and your willingness to be fully present to another person in his or her living. Here being fully present meant listening to stories of people's experience in a natural disaster.

What made such conversation pastoral? The people of the team went because they cared and they were willing to listen with discipline to those who had experienced the fires. We were all changed in some way as a result of the conversations we shared. We worked to make space for the people to talk about their lived experience in the fires. As they talked they were telling us about their souls. Their talk was not in religious language, and yet they attempted to name their lives in meaningful ways in face of the monstrous experience of the fires. To be present to people in this setting meant attending to people sharing deeply about terror they had experienced.

The people in the fires sometimes believed that as clergy we could frame this horrific event in such a way that took it into the presence of God. At the end of the day a clergy friend named John told how a couple walked him to a spot on their front lawn and said, "Our friend died here; would you please say a prayer?" They needed to tell the story to someone who could mark the sacredness of their experience.

When people go through distressing times, whether it is in this story of the fires or through crises such as losing a job, the breakup of a home, or the death of someone close, it is as though their bodies are ripped apart inside. When they are enabled to tell the story of their experience they are reintegrating their lives. Often they have to tell the story many times before they find healing. When they are enabled to tell what happened to someone who will listen with discipline, they are offered an opportunity to experience healing. This is pastoral conversation.

Tracy

Tracy was sixteen. Her mum asked me if I would be willing to have a conversation with Tracy. Tracy and I talked in my study for an hour and a half while her mum had a coffee in the lounge with my wife. The conversation was about Tracy's development as a sexual person and about choosing sexual values. At age sixteen, as young people are moving toward adulthood, two of the crucial things they need to address are their maturing sexuality and the development of their own value system as different from the value systems of their parents. It is a laborious transition.

Tracy told me that when her family had been on vacation in a caravan park she and her friend met some boys. The boys invited Tracy and her friend to their tent, and the girls accepted the invitation. The boys asked how far the girls wanted to go (sexually). Tracy said to them, "I don't want to go all the way because I'm not on the pill." The boy offered that he had "precautions," but Tracy said that she still did not want to go all away. She had, after all, only known this boy for about fifteen minutes. Over the next few nights when she saw this boy he was drunk, and he went off with another girl. The experience raised tough questions for an emerging woman: "Would he have liked me better if I had gone all the way?" "Did he get drunk and go off with someone else because I wouldn't have sex with him?"

In telling me this story Tracy had made herself vulnerable, sharing such intimate details about her own sexuality. I had known Tracy

15

a long time and we had a relationship of trust. The conversation had been growing over many years. As a way of valuing her sharing and of providing a base for our conversation to go deeper, I told of my own sexual values and choices in so far as they were relevant to supporting her in her choices. Then I gave her some information about differences between male and female sexuality, and told her that it was alright for her to say, "No." I informed her of her rights in any relationship. We talked together about how she would have felt if she had had sex with him and the same things had happened. Then we talked together about the risks of intimacy.

To help Tracy be clear about her own values I asked her to think about, and if she felt comfortable doing so, to articulate in what circumstances she would sleep with a person. She was very clear: "When I've known someone for a long time and feel very close to them." I affirmed this to be a most appropriate choice. And I encouraged Tracy in making such choices to be willing to hold out for this value. It is, I said, a matter of liking and looking after yourself. It is important to belong to a community like the church, because then you have a support group of people who like you and will tell you that you are alright, especially when you have an experience like this with a person who suggests that you are not.

In such conversations you have to be careful not to be a voyeur, careful not to be meeting your own sexual needs by listening to someone else's sexual experience, and careful to keep within appropriate boundaries agreed upon with parents of children who come for conversation.

In this conversation with Tracy we were thinking together about the goals or values that should undergird her living. She was thinking through ethical dilemmas that occur because she was now a sexual being and in relationship. When conversation addresses values or ethics in relationships or work or any other dimension of being, then it is pastoral.

Pat and Andrew

Pat and Andrew invited me to visit them. They had a seventeen-year-old son, Ian, with whom they were having some difficulty. In a conversation that lasted about an hour and a half, Pat and Andrew shared their pain, hurt, struggle, and anguish about parenting Ian.

I sat for long time thinking, "I don't know how to help you. I've been lucky, and I don't have a child like this. There's nothing I can do.

You've come to the wrong person." Even so, I sat and listened and trusted my imagination to respond with an appropriate image. Somewhere in the conversation, Andrew alluded to Deuteronomy 30:15ff, the story of Moses saying to the people, "This day you can choose life or you can choose death and I say to you choose life." In my head I made some connections. The connections were helped by the reading and thinking I'd done about what it means for people to move from being children to being adult in the context of their own family. In pastoral and psychological literature this is called "leaving home."

I had the sense that Pat and Andrew wanted Ian to be an independent adult and yet that he hooked them into accepting the ultimate responsibility for him and for his life. A couple of times Andrew suggested conditions under which Ian could live at home. I asked him, "Could you carry out your threat to ask Ian to leave?" He said, "No. I couldn't." Financially, Ian could not afford to leave home. He spent all the money that he earned, and when he ran out of money his parents were willing to support him. As I listened, I gleaned from this that Ian "hooks" Andrew and Pat into ultimately being responsible for his life. I also knew that Ian had threatened an attempt on his life. This is a tough place for parents to be. The possibility that a child, of whatever age, does not want the life that the parents have given causes the utmost distress. The parents will generally be willing to give up lots of their power to keep the child alive.

And so, aware that how questions are framed is really important, I asked Andrew and Pat, "Can you make Ian responsible for his own life?" "Yes, that's what we want to do." Then, I asked a much tougher, deeper question: "And his death?" It is a question I am not sure I would want people to ask me, and yet that seemed to be what was hooking Pat and Andrew; they had given their child life, and the child does not seem to want the life. This demands that they protect him against himself. That Ian does not want the life that Pat and Andrew have given him seems to them a judgment on them, and how they have given, nurtured, and shared with him that life.

To take the conversation forward, I drew on another metaphor of faith: "God gave his Son up to death, and only then could there be real and resurrected life." That is also very similar to the story of Abraham being asked to sacrifice Isaac and to the story of the waiting father who stands back and watches and waits anxiously for the return of his prodigal son.

I asked Andrew and Pat, "Can you make Ian responsible for his own death? If he wants to drink himself to death, if he wants to smoke himself to death, if he wants to starve himself to death, or if he wants to take other risks that will lead to his death, can you tell him in words and actions, that that is now his freedom? As parents, you will hurt intensely if he chooses death; on the other hand that is his freedom. Your cry is like Moses: "This day you can choose life or you can choose death, and I say to you choose life." The paradox of life is that people can only choose for something when they know they can choose against it too.

Andrew had described Ian's behavior as "becoming entrenched." I had kept that image in mind, remembering it and wondering how to use it. Instead of using it as a judgment to talk about the son, I asked the parents, "In what ways is *your* behavior entrenched?" I have come to understand that in families I can help the strong people, the ones with whom I am in conversation, to make changes; I cannot prescribe changes for an absent person. When one person in a family takes a different position from his or her usual one, then the other members have to adjust. So helping these parents take a different position could help their son behave differently. It is about the balance of the family. I suggested to Andrew that as a father, he could take a different position with Ian by taking the initiative to suggest that they do something adult together. Perhaps they could go to the football game and share a beer and conversation for an afternoon.

There is no doubt that my response or participation in this conversation was informed greatly by the reading and thinking I had done about young people leaving home. I was invited to be in the conversation because I was pastor to this family. While I drew on much that I had learned as a family therapist, I shaped that in the language of some key biblical stories. The Garden of Eden story, Moses and the people journeying in the wilderness, and the prodigal son/waiting father story all reflect something of the journey of leaving home, of becoming adult in the context of the family of origin.

Pastoral conversation is shaped in some significant ways because at least one of the participants is a theological interpreter who is open to hearing the voice of God in fresh and relevant ways that are beyond pious cliché.

A theological interpreter has the capacity to attend to both the human and existential experience of the people in his or her care and at the same time to the Christian tradition. Then, through an act of the imagination, the interpreter holds the two together, in ways that shape an ethic of care and justice.

A sermon as conversation

Earlier I recounted visiting with people at the time of the fires. In the strange synchronicity between faith and life, when it came to sermon preparation that week, I found the lectionary reading included Exodus 3:1–15, the story of Moses and the burning bush. A key part of this story is that the bush was burning and yet not consumed. In the sermon I talked about the devastation that the fires brought, and the transfixed look of the people who had been in the fires. I wondered with my congregation how we recognize the coming or the voice of God in this situation. I spoke of how God calls us to a new beginning, and that only in retrospect would we be able to say we were burned but not consumed. Then in the rebirth the people might recognize the transcendent moment that the fires brought. It would be a meeting with "I am who I am," about which they might ultimately be able to say, "We were burned but we were not consumed."

In the sermon I carried on the conversation begun when I was visiting the fire-ravaged area and I drew on the faith tradition by interpreting to the people how they might discern the voice of God in that difficult time. Theological reflection that doesn't use clichés or proof-texts to explain away difficult experience is a discipline that enriches pastoral conversation. It is brave to address God with life's hard questions. Theological reflection shapes pastoral conversation.

The workplace

Over the years I have visited many people in their workplaces. I want to say to them by my visit that I as their pastor am interested in what they do in their daily work. More than that, I want to confirm by my being with them that what they do in their daily work is ministry. Almost every time I go to someone's workplace people take me on a tour of the workplace and then sit down and tell me in a most businesslike way the ethical dilemmas they face in choosing to live out their faith in the workplace. These conversations move quickly into the "deeper places": passion for teaching, passion for looking after the environment, the desire to create a just society, commitment to care, and a desire to bring healing. Always people talk about their desire to be faithful as the people of God.

Conversation becomes pastoral when together people move into the deeper spaces and ask more ultimate questions about the purpose and meaning of life. It is pastoral when people together explore important questions about life and death, and about the nature of existence itself.

Tony

During one of my regular pastoral visits, Tony told me with some anticipation about a military reunion that he would attend in a few weeks. We talked together about the dilemmas of war, and of the strange twist in ethic that happens inside you: you are brought up being taught not to kill or hurt others; then "the state" instructs you to kill and hurt others, and then just as quickly makes you a civilian again, as which you are not to kill and hurt. We wandered around talking about this with not much focus to our conversation. It was what I would describe as chaotic. I didn't know where the conversation would lead. Then came a time of confession. Tony said, "I have never told anybody this," and then quietly told me stories of things he'd done in war. Difficult stories of difficult things done in difficult times. Things he had lived with silently for fifty years. Confession, fifty years on. How do I declare pardon and forgiveness? Tony had shared with me his deepest secrets. What is it like to be ordered to kill (at the threat of being killed yourself if you don't follow the order) to protect your nation in war? The stories were shared with me in trust and respect. As was my habit, I prayed with Tony. To this day I do not recall what words I said or how I assured him that he was forgiven and accepted by the grace of God, but from subsequent stories he told me, I surmised that he had experienced being forgiven.

Sometimes people in conversation move into spaces of chaos and not knowing where they are uncertain and even fearful. Somehow the voice of God breaks into these spaces and they find new life. In this encounter with Tony that chaos became the space for confession and a time for mediating the forgiveness of God. That is pastoral conversation.

Pastoral conversation describes all these situations, and more. When people are involved together in talk about the mission of God's church the conversation is pastoral. That is much of the business of the church: thinking together about how we will live responsibly the mission to which we are called. So, for example, a conversation with a volunteer teacher focusing the goals of a Sunday school class for young children is pastoral conversation. It works to shape the mission of the church.

I describe some others in the following text.

Awe-filled silence

A couple of men invited me on a mountain bike ride. We rode over some very rough terrain and I barely stayed on my bike. We climbed up a step incline over gravel ruts and rocks, then, puffing and panting, came to a large rock. We left our bikes and walked out to the precipice of a mighty valley. Hundreds of feet below a river quietly pushed on. We sat in silence for quite a while, speechless. We were in the presence of the mystery that is creation. We might just as easily have been in the presence of a newborn child or in an art museum. When, in the presence of life's mysteries, people sit together in respectful and awe-filled silence, that is pastoral conversation.

Richard

I went to visit Richard in his workplace. I went because I had heard his wife saying, "I don't know where I am in this marriage. I'm not sure whether I want to be in or out of the marriage. It's all a struggle for me." Richard's wife was signaling a crisis in which they both needed help. I took the initiative to talk with Richard. If I went to his workplace I was likely to have a conversation without interruptions from other members of the family. We went for lunch to a local pub. "I've come as a friend. If your spouse says that 'she's not sure where she is in the marriage,' it knocks you around. I'd like to give you an opportunity to talk about that." We talked about being parents of teenagers and of our sexuality and of our wives. We talked openly and frankly and Richard looked very emotional at times. When I left he walked with me to my car, and as I was leaving he reached through the window and touched me and very emotionally said, "Thanks for coming, I really appreciate this." "Blessings on you," I said, not sure how else to take my leave.

This action of his indicated how important and deep the conversation had been for him, reaching beyond language. I wanted to respond, but how? He was not pious, worshiped irregularly, and I was in my car about to leave. I responded with a blessing. Not a clear or confident blessing because I was a bit taken by surprise, but a blessing that wanted to say there had been a special quality of being in this conversation.

The blessing marked it as a pastoral conversation.

Alf and Merle

Alf was dying. I went to his home to share communion with him and his wife Merle. There was an elder with me representing the broader community of which we were a part. I have difficulty describing the conversation because so much of the intensity and the intimacy lay in what was not said. Alf told me that he was not able to read, except for the "Holy Book." As he told me this, he burst into tears and then was embarrassed that he couldn't control the tears. We shared communion and he cried again. Alf wanted me to explain his tears. How would I respond? I was uncertain, and said, "They are natural, God-given. There is an emotional pain for you in this journey (and I named some of those emotional pains) as well as the physical pain. With emotional pain your body tightens and the tears release the tension, enabling you to relax. Jesus also cried when faced with the agony of the cross." I pointed to the bread and wine on the table and said, "Somehow, in some mysterious way, Jesus' tears and our tears mix together as we share the bread and wine." "Thank you for explaining that. It is helpful," he said.

Conversations sometimes go where words cannot easily reach, where the symbols speak of mysteries beyond our easy comprehension. That is pastoral conversation.

The communion shared with Alf and Merle was also an intensified conversation. I had shared cake and tea with them in their home many times. This day the circumstance was different. We used bread and wine rather than tea and cake. We knew that Alf's life would end soon. We knew that Merle would walk a lonely path saying good-bye to her husband of many years. The intensification made the conversation sacred. Together we were open to being addressed by the Divine.

Pastoral conversation is made sacred by its recognition that this ordinary thing, conversation, can be entered openly and deeply. When conversation is thus entered, the being of the other is held up, valued, and acknowledged before God, in blessing, prayer, or some other symbolic act.

Earlier I talked about my difficulty in people asking me to pray for them. They saw in me, and were acknowledging to me, that I am a symbolic representative of God. I didn't see that for myself and so I let them down. In almost every conversation that I have recounted in this chapter there is an expectation of me as a representative of God. In asking the question about his tears, Alf wanted a pastoral, not simply psychological, answer and so it was appropriate to link his tears with those of Jesus. In my role as minister I broke bread and shared wine with him. In whatever circumstance, when we engage in conversation as pastoral people there is an expectation that we are representatives of God.

We are not all capable of doing all these things. Certainly none of us does all of them all of the time. Motivated by a desire to share Christ's love, we do some of these things some of the time, and do them falteringly, uncertainly at that. We do them hoping that when we do we will acknowledge the living of others, make better relationships, better communities, and better societies. We hope that we will enact the ministries to which we are called. We hope that in a small way through our care, we will bring healing, hope, and an awareness of God's lively presence in the world.

So far in this book we have established that conversation is pastoral when there is a desire to care, when people attend to and listen to the other with discipline, and when that listening is about the living of the other. And ultimately, the conversation is open to moving into the space of the sacred or the divine through its intensification of the ordinary.

How do you engage in such conversations? How do you know what to say and when to say it? How do you listen? How do you take the conversation deeper? How do you be present to what is happening so that you can name and celebrate the presence of God? How do you name and celebrate the conversation as pastoral? How do you become a pastoral person? It is to these questions that the next chapters turn.

Discipline

The discipline needed to shape pastoral conversation is similar to the discipline needed to shape the other things we do.

I love to draw. I draw whenever I can: in meetings, at weddings, on the train station, at jazz concerts. I carry a sketchbook everywhere.

It is part of being an artist and I work really hard at it. Often when people see me drawing for the first time, they look at the drawings and say, "You are so lucky to have that gift. I wish I could do that." I tell them that when I began I wasn't very good. I didn't begin drawing until I was about thirty, but I have drawn almost every day since. Each week I spend two hours drawing the human figure from life. I can do it *because I do it*.

There seems to be a common assumption about drawing that it is totally gift and no discipline. Yet it is mostly discipline. The same assumption seems to exist about being in conversation; people think you either have the skills or you don't. Like drawing, if you have the desire and the discipline, I am convinced you will be able to engage in significant pastoral conversation.

If as you read these stories you find yourself saying, "I'd like to be able to do that," know that you can. You will need to give it time and energy, for it requires discipline.

The next chapters

In these chapters I have broken conversation into many parts, which if practiced can improve your capacity to engage others in deep, open conversation. All the parts seem to me to be important in making conversation. You can be aware of them and not aware of them at the same time. It is a bit like someone coaching you on how to make a good swing at golf or tennis. They break the swing down into all its component parts and encourage you to focus on just one of those parts at a time when you practice. If you tried to attend to all that they said about the swing at the same time your body would freeze up, and you wouldn't be able to hit a single ball. If you attend to one small thing at a time, if you are aware of it, practice it, adjust your stance, adjust your grip, then your swing improves and you hit the ball further, harder, and more accurately.

So by all means read through and think about all the parts that contribute to conversation, but when engaging in conversation start out by being aware of and practicing only one or two things at a time. When you find something works, then it becomes a resource for your next conversation.

PREPARING FOR THE CONVERSATION

THE BEGINNING POINT: LOVE THE PEOPLE

An older minister whom I admired was returning to parish ministry after a long period as a resource person for the national church. I asked how he planned to make the transition. "I will love the people given to my care," he responded simply. It was for me a ministry-shaping conversation. I had never before heard articulated this call to people in pastoral ministry. From that day to this, it has been one of my primary goals in ministry to love the people given to my care. Everything else builds on this. It is the beginning point for pastoral conversation, and this openness to love the people will shape our being formed for pastoral ministry.

PREPARATION

Christian ministry begins with an openness to being shaped by your faith through being grounded in Christian community and the practices of Christian faith. Reading in the Christian tradition (Bible, theology, spirituality, and so forth) along with worship, prayer, and reflection together form the crucible in which pastoral conversation is shaped. Engaging these disciplines as a lifelong practice will shape and enable you to engage in pastoral conversation.

OPENNESS TO LEARNING ABOUT LIFE

Be willing to learn about life. When you experience something that is different, be aware of it, write about it, and reflect on it. What you learn will shape how you relate to others. Such learning will equip you to engage in deep conversation with people in diverse settings.

Mark

Mark asked if he could come and talk with me. He had suffered a major brain hemorrhage after a drinking binge at age nineteen that had left him in a coma for three months. With good therapy and determination he had managed to live alone again. He was a brave and wise man who could say, "I'm glad this happened, because if it hadn't I'd be dead from alcohol poisoning." He told me of his experience while in the coma. I learned from Mark what I could never have learned in a textbook: that some people in a coma are aware of what is happening around them and that I ought to relate to them on that assumption. Conversation has been one source for my learning about life. Reading books and journals, watching movies, reading the daily paper, going to the theater, listening to music in an open and reflective way are among the other things that have also been helpful.

Neale

My pastor friend Neale lived through intense and frightening fires in his suburb. He knew that, like him, the community was in shock. He had enough confidence to know that the material he had prepared for worship on the following Sunday morning would be totally irrelevant. Trusting what he had learned about life from many sources, he knew that the people in his community would need to talk about their experience. So at worship he invited people to tell the stories of what their experience had been in the last twenty-four hours. Yet he was somewhat uncertain about doing this: Would it be appropriate? Would the people appreciate it? Would it be helpful? It turned out to be most appropriate, and it showed that Neale had learned much about life and what people needed in the circumstance. He created the space for a pastoral conversation in the context of worship.

How else might you learn about life? Read the literature that draws on the others' knowledge and informs your own knowing of human experience. A couple were to see me to talk about their relationship. All I had gleaned was that "Jimmy was violent." I didn't know much about domestic violence, so I looked up an article on domestic violence that I had read in a family therapy journal. The article gave me information that I hadn't known and helped me engage the conversation in a more appropriate way.

Reflection

Another way to learn about life is to reflect with discipline on your own experience. I learned a lot about being a parent by reflecting on my experience of being parented. It was eerie as a parent to be outside of my body watching my parent act in me. I was doing to my children what my parents had done to me. Learning from that meant that I could choose a different parenting model. Similarly, you might reflect on your experience with others. Every conversation, every experience you share provides knowledge that will inform new conversations and experiences that you have.

Disciplined reflection builds a store of wisdom about life. The daily discipline of keeping a journal helps this reflective process. All the stories in this book come from my daily journal where I have written about pastoral experience in a reflective way that will inform my future conversation.

After engaging in a conversation you might want to try your hand at this kind of journaling, and take some time to write about it. Be specific. Name what happened, be descriptive. How did you feel? In what ways were you helpful or unhelpful in the conversation? What questions emerged that address you and your life situation? What questions emerged for you that you might have to spend more time reading or reflecting upon? How will your pastoral ministry be shaped as a result of this conversation? How does this experience bring questions to the biblical text that you might be preaching upon or listening to next week? How will your prayer be influenced by this conversation?

INTENTIONALITY

To be good at pastoral conversation you have to be intentional. That means knowing what you want to do, knowing how you will do it, and going about it in a focused way. The things that we do well are most often the things we have thought about and planned. In the same way pastoral conversations have to be set up, thought about, prepared for, and planned.

MAKING APPOINTMENTS

Being intentional will include making appointments for conversation. I recall the time when my father-in-law died suddenly. At the time my parents were making a rare visit from inter-state to stay with us in our home. I was engaged in a most significant conversation with my father, as you can only do on the morning after your wife's father has died. The doorbell rang. A minister had called to visit. The conversation with my father was, for me, distressingly interrupted; even more significantly, my wife wasn't home. The minister thought that she had done her job simply in calling; we engaged in no significant conversation and she never called back to see my wife. After the minister had gone, my father, a former salesman who had always had to be most intentional about his conversation, commented: "That person didn't want to be successful in what she was doing." He talked about her lack of intention. Her inability to phone ahead was reflected in her inability to focus the conversation.

How might the conversation have been different for us and for her? A phone call to say: "I have heard that your father/father-in-law has died. I'd like to call in. When would be a convenient time?" could have allowed us to prepare for her visit, ensured that my wife could be present, and permitted me to complete the conversation with my father. It also would have given us time to think through what we wanted from this pastoral conversation in the time of distress.

Phoning and making appointments to visit allows the other participants in the conversation to have "power" in determining a suitable time and preparing for what they want to happen in conversation with their pastoral person. Often I hear my colleagues saying they'd rather call spontaneously and that the surprise element is important in the conversation. I think that is self-deceptive. The important thing is giving other people an opportunity to prepare for and think through what they want from the conversation. The surprise element (turning up unexpectedly) in conversation protects the pastoral person from ever being "not in control" of the conversation.

Jim

Our parish included a cluster of congregations, each with its own minister. One of my clergy colleagues was away and I was phoned and asked to visit Jim in his stead. When I phoned I got a fairly negative response. I could hear Jim's daughter holding the phone away and whispering, "It's Doug Purnell from Lakeside Church." The response came back, "No, he doesn't want you to come. He's just come back from the doctor's." I sought to make a time that would be convenient for Jim and was told to phone back in a few days. I felt hurt, pushed aside, even though I respect the right of people to say, "No thanks." Some concerned members of the congregation asked me to phone again in a few days, which I did. The phone was not answered. I was ready to give up. Certainly I was not in control of the conversation at this stage.

A congregational elder contacted me to relay that Jim was embarrassed that he had responded to me so brusquely. He really would like me to go and see him.

Jim was now in hospital. When I walked in he was asleep, and the nurse woke him gently. He had to work hard to get the words out. First an appreciation for my coming, and then an apology and explanation for the brusqueness. None was needed. I ought to understand that people who have been told they are terminally ill need space and can be hurting and angry. Yet my phone calls allowed him to have the conversation on his terms and when he was ready.

I asked Jim, "How are you inside?" He raised himself, eventually slipping his legs over the side of the bed so that he could sit up and talk with me. "That could mean two things," he said, "physically or mentally?" And he proceeded to tell me slowly, deliberately, with effort, his eyes at times rolling behind closed lids. "Physically, I have cancer of the pancreas. The Christian doctor, who some don't like because he is too blunt, sat me down and told me in great detail that he can't operate. Then he outlined other forms of treatment that he wouldn't recommend because of the side-effects. 'What's left?' I asked the doctor, 'To bat out time?' 'Yes,' the doctor said. 'Palliative care. Drug therapy to relieve the pain.' 'How much time?' I asked. 'Two months.'

"Mentally, I know what's going on. I'm alright. But I worry for Beth; I always thought I would go first."

There was a lament. Jim talked about his seventy-seven-year-old body. The doctor had asked him, "Do you smoke?" "No." "Do you drink?" "No." "Have you had diabetes?" "No." And so on. "Had a hip replacement, that's all." The question for him was not "Why should this happen to me?" but "Why should it happen to my body when I have been so healthy?"

Then followed a deep and intimate conversation about how you face your own death, the fear of pain, the recognition of unconsciousness, the role and place of drugs. He was particularly concerned about how to say good-bye to his wife and family. "Will we be together at that moment when I am called or will we be apart? How will I know I'm being called?" (Not in the sense of missing the call; rather, will I be drugged, will I just fade away not aware of the moment?) I told Jim that my previous experience with people who have been close to death and haven't died was that the unconsciousness takes away the pain, and it seems like you have an experience similar to dreaming. In the "dream" you have a sense of the call coming.

I asked Jim, "How will you say good-bye to your wife?" He said, "We haven't worked anything out," and went on to say he would probably be unconscious at that time. In my family was a story about how important it would be to talk about this together. I told Jim how my mum had died of cancer when I was seven years old. In an adult conversation, my father told me how the doctor had said, "Don't tell your wife that she is dying." Years later he thought that was the stupidest advice, because they went through this long time not talking about her dying. Tears began to trickle down Jim's face.

I suggested that Jim might take an hour with his wife while he was conscious: shut the door, have the nurses dissuade other visitors, sit together as husband and wife and talk about what it means to acknowledge the fifty-plus years together. Maybe take an hour to sit quietly and say nothing, and maybe say the things you aren't sure you'll be able to say later. "That's helpful," he said.

When I'd been there about an hour Jim seemed to have said many of the things that he needed to say. He was getting tired. I offered a few things: I would come and sit with him in the following weeks. He didn't have to talk to me if he didn't feel like talking. I'd be happy to sit. He accepted the offer. And I said I would visit his wife and give her some support. He had a Bible beside the bed and I asked what Bible passages were important to him. Psalm 121, Psalm 23, and he attempted to get out another but ran out of energy, and I left. If he'd had more energy, I might have offered to read one of these Psalms, but that could wait for another day.

The intriguing thing in this conversation was that Jim, who first resisted my initiative to visit, really had so much to talk about. And he came to the conversation in his time, when he was ready. Phoning ahead enabled him to prepare for this important conversation.

Convenience—yours or theirs?

Phoning ahead and giving people time to prepare for your visit is also important in these times of heightened awareness of sexual harassment. The spontaneous visit may well be discerned as an inappropriate visit. You always need to leave people the space to say, "This is not an appropriate time for a visit." Inappropriately timed visits may be interpreted as harassment. In a later section we will look more closely at what is appropriate and inappropriate in conversation.

Yet making appointments and phoning ahead is hard work. I didn't find it easy to receive the "No thanks," from Jim. Sometimes I had a free afternoon, with nothing planned, so I'd decide to visit. On one such afternoon I phoned and asked if it was convenient. I was told, "No" and we made a time for three weeks hence. What they didn't understand was that I had time now! Spending time making appointments is demanding work and important in creating the environment for significant pastoral conversation. Whether you are lay or ordained it is beneficial to ask, "When would be a convenient time?"

Pam

On the other hand, of course there are conversations that are spontaneous, that happen because you are there. Just after Christmas I was in line at the supermarket. I stood next to Pam who worked in the local butcher shop and whom I saw there each week. "Did you have a good Christmas," I asked. Her face fell, her demeanor became heavy. "No, it was very sad." "Sad?" I asked. "Yes," she said, "my brother died. He was only fifty. Too young to die." The general preparation and thinking that shapes all the other conversations shaped this conversation too.

Expectation and anxiety

Even when the pastoral person has made an appointment to visit with people, the people are often uncertain as to what they might expect from the conversation, unlike a visit from an electrician or other service person. I've often been so obsessed with my own fears about the visit (What will these people be like? Will they like me? Will their theology be like mine or . . . ? What will they offer me to drink?) that

I haven't always been so conscious of people's nervous anticipation of *my* visit: (What will he be like? Will he judge us? Will he like our home? What does he want? What have we done? Will he like what we offer him to eat?) So when the visit happens there can be a lot of anxiety floating around—as there was on my first visit to Sue and Lee.

Sue and Lee

One evening I visited Sue, who had been coming to church alone. At their home I met her husband, Lee, who was not sympathetic to the church and wanted to know, "Why are you here? What have we done?" That wasn't an unusual response when I visited people for the first time. I explained that it was an expectation of the church that the minister would visit everyone in the congregation periodically. "Through my visit, I want to say to you both that I am interested in who you are, interested in your life." Both said that it hadn't been their experience to be visited by a minister before. Their questions reflected their anxiety and uncertainty about my visit. Because they were open about these questions it was possible to make a genuine and appropriate connection that was far more significant than if they had been "nice and polite" with me.

The big anxiety most people have is that the pastoral people visiting are "religious" and therefore have the moral high ground, and those being visited are likely to be "judged." Nobody wants to be in conversation with someone who will stand in judgment of them. With Sue and Lee, saying clearly why I had come to see them alleviated their fear of the purpose of my visit. It helped that I had thought about who they were and what they might be anticipating from my visit before I went to their home.

ATTENDING TO PEOPLE'S LIFE STAGES

Another way to prepare for the conversation is to be aware of who the people are with whom you are going to talk or visit. What do you know of their experience of life? How can you invite them to talk about that? Sometimes we think we should be protecting people from their own emotion. In fact they don't need protection; they need someone who will give them the opportunity to talk. But how do you do that? How do you ask a new widower what it is like living in the house on his own or the recently separated person how she is getting on?

Francis

Francis had recently separated from his wife of many years. He had moved to a new town and into rented accommodation. Because of the difficulties involved in coming to a financial settlement, he lived on little money and his apartment was sparsely furnished. "What is it like being on your own?" I asked. And he told me, but it wasn't an easy flowing conversation, it was emotional and rambling. Since I had some idea about what happens to people after separation I could shape my questions and my listening around his present experience.

If you don't know the person's particular life experience you can nevertheless be aware of where are they in the life cycle. Are they newly married? Young parents? Parents of teenagers? Empty-nesters? People approaching death? Recently widowed? Where people are in the life cycle will frame different existential questions. Betty Carter and Monica McGoldrick's book *The Extended Family Life Cycle* (1999), journals, and the Web will inform you about the various stages of life and help shape your conversations.

EXPECTATION

In preparing for a conversation it is helpful to ask, "What does this person expect from me?"

He didn't pray

It is realistic to expect that when I call the plumber to my home he or she will know about pipes and drains and sewage and have some technical skills to address and rectify associated problems. What sorts of competencies and knowledge might a person expect from a pastoral person? Even when people know what they want, they are uncertain how to ask. A lay member in my local church recounted an ordained person's visit to her home: "The minister came and visited; I appreciated the conversation. I wanted him to pray with me and he didn't." She expressed her disappointment. He didn't offer and she didn't ask.

How could this pastor have been aware of the expectation that he would offer to pray? The pastoral person has to accept responsibility for shaping the conversation, for giving it focus through an awareness of the need of the other. Asking questions such as "How are you?" "Will you tell me about . . . ?" "What is happening at your work?" and so on helps bring focus and avoid a feeling of boredom and anxiety.

A friend of mine simply asks those he visits to tell him about their lives—and they do.

When people talk about their lives, when they tell the stories of their experience, they are saying who they are. They are naming themselves, telling their identity. When they tell the story of their own living in a meaningful way they are talking about their souls. That is what the stories in this book are about: people naming their identity, talking about their souls in order that they might live more abundantly the grace of God. People might expect that their pastoral person will listen to their living without judgment, they might expect to be heard in their own language (remember Bruce Gostelow.) They might expect that when the conversation goes where it seems there are no adequate words, their pastoral person will be quiet and re-spectful. They might expect that their pastoral person will be willing to move into the silences and wait for appropriate images and words to emerge. They could expect a caring conversation partner to find a resonance and reverberation with the stories of faith. They could ex-pect their pastoral person to be open to identifying the voice of God emerging in fresh ways. They could expect that the conversation will go to the space of deep prayer. Simply put, they could expect you to listen while they tell you something of who they are and their expe-rience of life. And you will have fulfilled a pastoral function if you lis-ten openly and with discipline.

Integrating life

In talking about their living people could expect help from you in in-tegrating the painful and discordant experiences of their lives, and to talk meaningfully about their major life transitions. They could ex-pect to share their celebrations and hopes. They could expect to talk about the content of their faith and be helped by you to clarify and name the things they believe. They could expect help in naming their life goals and values. They could expect help in thinking through eth-ical decisions. They could expect help in theological reflection and they could expect that you would acknowledge their mutual faith in some helpful way.

They may not be able to name these things, but that doesn't mean they don't want them. A significant pastoral skill, worth developing, may be to discern what the people do want from the conversation. I like how Jesus could ask Blind Bartimaeus (Mark 10:46–52), "What do you want me to do for you?" When he heard clearly Bartimaeus' expectation, he could respond appropriately.

The agenda

I had an ongoing conversation with a woman over a number of weeks. I struggled in the conversation. This person seemed depressed and not moving. I seemed unable to help. At Christmas I was most surprised when this woman gave me a small gift, some dark chocolates, and a card with a Picasso drawing, on which she written, "Thank you for a place to 'curse the darkness!'" What a wonderful way to name a difficult conversation. The gift suggested that I had misread the significance of the conversation for her. People take from conversation what they want and sometimes what they take is very different from what I think I am giving. How could I have understood better what she wanted and got from the conversation?

When Jesus talked with Bartimaeus he could clearly ask about and respond to Bartimaeus' agenda. Ask whose agenda is important in a conversation. It is possible to be involved and responsible for shaping a conversation without controlling the agenda of that conversation. When I function as a therapist, a simple way to begin is to ask the other person, "What do you hope to get from this conversation?" Then I can work to clarify their expectations. If I know what they want I can work to help them achieve it.

In conversation it is so easy for the pastoral person to set and control the agenda. The effect of controlling the agenda is that it keeps the conversation at a "surface" level where it remains safe and free from any emotional demand. Being open to the agenda of the other is very important. It isn't so easy to ask, "What do you hope to get from this conversation?" in the informal settings in which most conversation takes place. Yet if you are open, people will tell you. I called a friend after a tragic accident in which a number of young people were killed. My friend's son was "lucky" in that he got out alive. The friend asked, "You don't mind if I tell you the story, do you? I've got to tell someone." He knew his own need and was able to clearly name his own agenda for the conversation. Often this desire to tell a clergy person or a representative of the church is a way of telling God.

PRAY FOR THE PEOPLE

Pray for the people you will engage in conversation. Most simply, hold an awareness of the people before God. I wish that I had great and wise things to say about how I prayed for people before conversations. I don't. Conversation always seemed to me to move toward the space of prayer when I might be able to shape a prayer. As I drove to people's homes, as I walked up their path, as I went into their workplaces, as I sat in a coffee shop there would be a time of anticipation, a moment of uncertainty when I wondered what might come from the conversation. In that moment I would be aware of the person I was to meet with and aware of God. I would seek to hold the two together. Somehow that is how I prayed for people. Others I'm sure have more focused practices.

SUMMARY

In preparing for conversations, live with discipline the practices of faith so that you will be formed as a person of faith. Love the people given to your care. Be open to learning about life from what you can read and from what you experience. Be intentional. Think ahead into the conversation. Do appropriate preparation. Think about where people are in the life cycle. Make appointments with people that allow space for them to prepare for what they want from the conversation. Be open to the agenda the other person will bring to the conversation. Be open to the expectations people will have of you as a pastoral person. And pray for the people.

5

THE WHERE, WHEN, AND WHO
OF PASTORAL CONVERSATION

Where do pastoral conversations take place? Who initiates them? And how long should they last?

THE SETTING FOR PASTORAL CONVERSATION

Where does pastoral conversation take place? It seems obvious to answer "everywhere," but I think that it needs some clarifying.

Jesus' conversation

It seems that all the recorded conversations of Jesus with the people of his community took place in "their" space. He spoke to them where he met them, most often in the public space, and in certain circumstances he accepted invitations into their homes to engage in specific conversation. He called Zacchaeus down from the tree and asked him to take him home (Luke 19:1ff). He met Levi sitting in his office (Luke 5:27ff). He went to the home of Simon the Pharisee (Luke 7:36ff), and shared the Passover meal in the house of an acquaintance (Mark 14:12ff). If we are enacting pastoral conversation as followers of Jesus we might follow his model of moving into the space of the other. When people are in their own space they are much more comfortable and secure and more able to engage deeper questions.

The space of the people

The majority of the stories of conversations shared in this book have taken place in the other person's space. In one parish where I was in ministry we had a drop-in senior citizens program. Our center was beside a state housing estate where thirty-five hundred people lived in high-rise apartments on ten acres. One housing block alone comprised two hundred single efficiency rooms. The people who lived here were mostly elderly and many came to our church for lunch. In those small rooms with a bed and a chair, a table and a TV, the people were all most comfortable to talk about their lives. I would sit and eat lunch with them at the church and go away regularly for weekends with them. The serious life-shaping conversations always took place in their apartments, where the symbols of their lives were around them and where they felt secure enough to say the deeper things.

We might have vastly different conversations if we were to follow Jesus' example and move into the other person's space. Visit the homes, workplaces, and recreational centers of people and meet them in ways that are at once ordinary and sacred. Meet with them where they live and work, in their spaces, and hear their stories. The conversation will be markedly different for your having taken the initiative to meet people in their spaces.

Tony

Tony was a colleague, a community youth worker. We shared an office for a few years. He was outstanding at his job. He spent a good part of his time in pinball parlors with young people. Many would disparagingly say, "What a cushy job." Tony could easily have been seduced to engage the "play" of the young people and forgotten his function as a youth worker. He didn't. He knew clearly his function and was there to engage specific and intentional conversation with young people, which involved careful listening and appropriate and thoughtful response. It was demanding work.

Pastoral conversation can happen anywhere. In these diverse places and times the pastoral person has to be alert to his or her particular identity and role, to know what makes a conversation pastoral, and to be willing to intentionally engage in a conversation as a pastoral person. It can flow from the casual, "How are you?" asked of someone in the parking lot, who responds to the question at a deeper level, "Since you ask, I am struggling. We are having to find a nursing home for my mother, who is no longer able to care for herself." It may be the more intentionally focused home visit following an accident. In every circumstance it is the preparedness and openness of the caring person that will transform the ordinary into something decidedly pastoral through his or her ability to focus the moment.

The public space

Whenever I can, I invite people into public spaces, such as coffee shops, for it reinforces that we belong together as community. It is sometimes easier, less threatening to me, and more equal for both of us to engage in conversation over a drink somewhere. Seeing people as a pastor in my office means that I am acting more like a counselor (with the attendant power) than a pastoral person. Sitting with a person over a cup of coffee, where I can ask exactly the same questions, is more likely to be experienced as valuing the other as equal and as friend. For me as a male, I am less comfortable having intimate conversations with women, particularly those of my age, in their homes; it is both more comfortable and safer to have deeper conversations in a public setting.

Telephone: Mary

The telephone is another vehicle for pastoral conversation. Mary phoned to tell about the sudden death of her mother. As she talked, she told me a story. She had been breast-feeding her young daughter after breakfast. The daughter had finished on one breast and was playing on the other, putting her finger on her mother's nipple, and then to her mouth. Mary was aware that it was a time of play. The daughter had had her breakfast before and this was a supplement that she didn't really need. Because she was just playing, the mother put her on the floor. The daughter screamed loudly, not because she was hungry but because this right to be with her mum was taken from her. Mary said with tears: I realized that is just what has happened with my mum and me. People find it easier to say the deeper things in metaphors. This simple and profound metaphor came in the phone conversation informing me of Mary's mother's death. It was appropriate to listen and respond in the moment. A couple of hours later I went to visit Mary in her home where we continued the conversation begun on the phone.

Generally, I'm not a good telephone person. I'm often brusque when people phone me, and I'm particularly reluctant to talk on the phone with people I don't know closely about the deep and precious parts of my life. Yet, when I do know people well, the phone has been a great way to have a deep conversation. Of course, it's also a great way to make contact, to check up on the community, to share information, to follow up on a concern and take a conversation deeper. When my wife took a phone call recently she remarked to the caller, "You sound a bit low today." "I've just lost my job," came the response, and a deeper conversation followed.

In the car

I choose to travel to meetings of the Presbytery with a fellow minister. In is our time of "catching up." "How is your family?" I ask. He tells me then that he will become a new grandfather. "Your married daughter?" I ask. "No, my unmarried son." Then follows a conversation about what happens when our children choose different values from their parents. We have an uninterrupted hour in the car for this conversation. The car is also a place for conversation that is not threatening, that values the other equally, that is typically free from interruption, and that provides the space for longer rolling conversations that inevitably go deeper.

INITIATING PASTORAL CONVERSATION

If conversation can happen anywhere, how does one initiate pastoral conversation?

Tell me about your life

The first phase of pastoral conversation is to make contact in order that you can know the person. Having prepared yourself for the conversation and having made contact, begin simply. Don't be in a hurry. When it seems appropriate you can ask people general questions. Asking "How long have you lived here?" or "Tell me about your life" will get you started.

Where the person being visited is in the life cycle might suggest times to initiate conversation and appropriate questions to ask in the conversation. If you are uncertain it might shape focused reading. If a family's children are being married, that might be an appropriate time to visit and be in conversation about what this transition in life may mean for them. If somebody is about to be laid off, retire from work, change significant jobs, or the like these might mark particular times, particular changes, particular transitions when a caring conversation might be much appreciated.

From this beginning point almost anything provides the opportunity to initiate a conversation. Here are a few suggestions:

- Key events in people's lives (birth, marriage, death, geographic movement, illness, hospitalization, graduation, being laid off work),

- When you are aware that people are going through hard times at work, at home, in relationships,

- When people are making tough decisions about jobs, ethics, movement, family, a relationship and so on,

- When someone asks,

- When you observe unusual things in people's behavior,

- When someone in the community says, "I think Jane would appreciate a visit" or "I am worried about Richard; he seems distracted at the moment."

How do you know with whom to be in conversation? Working closely with elders or leaders means that you will very quickly learn who needs to be visited. Having a time of sharing "pastoral concerns" within the elders' council or pastoral leaders' meeting alerts one to pastoral needs and people who need to be visited.

LEARNING GROUPS AS A PLACE OF SHAPING CONVERSATION

Conversation doesn't have to be one-to-one. It can happen in groups. When I thought a number of people in the community were asking similar questions about life, I used that as an opportunity to organize a group where a focused conversation could take place.

Nathan and the youth group

One such group conversation occurred when George died suddenly. He was the father of Nathan, who was a member of our youth group. I wanted to help the young people know how to talk with Nathan about his dad's death. I wanted Nathan to know that we were taking him and the death of his dad very seriously. To say, "We are praying for you," had to be more than mere words. I hoped that all the young people would learn something about how to live with life and death and how to pray deep prayer.

Knowing that Nathan would be present, I told him what I wanted to do this night, and why I thought it important. He thought it appropriate and was willing to be present.

We had gathered in the church hall, and when the time was appropriate, I gathered the young people together and told them of Nathan's dad's death. Most already knew.

I told the young people some things about death. Death hurts. Emotions bubble within us. We get scared. We cry. We put ourselves in the situation and we don't know how we'd cope if the same thing happened to us. I personalized these things as much as I could. I looked at Nathan and said, "When I learned that your dad died, Nathan, I cried. When I came to your home and met your family, I cried. My glasses steamed up and tears rolled down my face. I opened my mouth to say something and no words came out."

In a group it is always important to talk directly to individual people, rather than about them as though they were not there. I wanted to model to young people how to give a direct message to someone who is hurting. Then I told them about how important it is to care and how easy in the circumstances to want to stay away. Touching people appropriately can be important when you don't know what words to say.

I structured a way for all those present to say something directly to Nathan. I asked them each to write a personal message to Nathan on a piece of paper, then we'd collect those messages, paste them in a book, and give the book to Nathan. "Write what you feel and what you wish for Nathan. It can be a very simple statement: 'I care,' 'I feel helpless.' And what other words are appropriate for you. Sign your name." We took all the messages and pasted them into a book and gave the book to Nathan. And then as a group we gave Nathan a community hug—a way of saying together, "We care."

This conversation constructed with the youth group happened in one meeting. At other times I organized groups of people to meet weekly for six weeks to have conversations about work, our vision for the future, our experience of pain, parenting, and so on. In the groups I asked lots of questions about people's experience of living. Through the questions I could initiate and shape intentional pastoral conversations involving a number of participants. In these groups people could have large slabs of time to address the questions and then equally large slabs of time to "tell their story." When they shared their stories with others in the group they were creating a quality community.

Further examples of questions that might help focus particular conversations are outlined in chapters 12–19.

LENGTH OF CONVERSATION

If you know where pastoral conversation takes place and you have some ideas about initiating pastoral conversation, how long should you allow for the conversation?

The conversations I've recounted in this book ranged from five minutes to two hours; some took place over the course of several months. The needs of the person(s) and the situation(s) in which they find themselves influence the amount of time that would be appropriate to have a conversation. Both your needs and their needs are important here. Sometimes pastors rush in and rush out in a hurry to get somewhere else and the people they have been talking with express a frustration that the conversation wasn't long enough for them to say anything.

The time and location where the conversation takes place will affect its length. If the conversation is in a hospital, twenty minutes might seem a long time, and if the conversation is in a home, twenty minutes might seem rude. I find that making one hour available is a reasonable amount of time to engage in good conversation, whether it be in home, office, coffee shop, or some other place. An hour might be good in white middle-class homes and considered rude in some other cultural groupings. A pastoral conversation in Tonga or Hawaii will have a decidedly different form from a similar conversation in Australia or the United States.

Work out for yourself what is an appropriate time to achieve what you want from a conversation. If you run into someone in the street, five minutes might be plenty; to visit a home an hour might be helpful; to intentionally work helping someone think about his or her marriage might need longer still. Understand, too, that conversations never really finish. They continue the next time that you meet and they build on previous meetings.

SUMMARY

Pastoral conversation can happen anywhere and anytime if the caring person is open to the opportunity. It can last from a few minutes to a couple of hours depending on the circumstance. The place in which the conversation takes place can shape the conversation. The preparedness and openness of the caring person will transform the ordinary into something decidedly pastoral through his or her ability to focus the moment.

6

MOVING INTO THE CONVERSATION

Edie

I went to visit Edie in her flat. She was a widow living alone. The reason for the visit was to say, "You are an important part of our community, and I'd like to get to know you a little." I knocked on the grey door and was ushered in and offered one of the two chairs in the room. Edie went to her kitchenette to make me a cup of tea. I looked around the room uncertainly. What will I talk with her about? My eyes fixed on a wedding photograph. I thought that was safe, so as a way of connecting or joining with Edie I asked if it was her wedding photo. I was surprised at the speed and honesty of her response. "No, that is my daughter. When I got married I was pregnant. I wasn't allowed to be married in the church. The wedding took place in the vestry and there were no photographs." Under my breath I uttered an expletive at the sadness of that. My attempt to join Edie in the conversation had gone much deeper than I imagined. It meant our conversation was deep and rich from the outset.

JOINING AND MAKING CONTACT

In any conversation an appropriate part of the process is to "join" with the other. This most often involves the greeting and acknowledgment of the other person and his or her surroundings and life.

The publican

When you don't know someone you look for all sorts of ways to make contact. I was having dinner in a pub with a friend. He introduced me to the publican, who was sitting at the bar eating his meal. He had the logo of his football club on his shirt, so I could ask about that. We began to talk. The conversation stayed on the surface, and that was appropriate. In someone's home or office there are usually photos or objects, symbols of the people's lives that allow you a way to begin talking together. In some settings and cultures we join by checking out who people know, who their family members are, where they have lived. All these things begin the process of giving identity to the other and enabling us to know how to relate with that person. Effectively joining with another person is essential to taking conversation deeper.

It is tough when you spend your time and energy trying to "join" or make contact with another person who for whatever reason doesn't reciprocate. I was at a wedding reception and sitting next to someone I had not known. I've had similar conversations in various settings. I asked lots of questions about him, where he lived, what work he did, how many children he had, where he goes for vacation. The conversation didn't go anywhere; neither did the person reciprocate by asking me similar questions. Those conversations are hard work and they remain superficial.

In the joining phase of conversations there is sometimes an awkward time where you are polite and agree, even though you disagree with every fiber of your being. You do this in order that you can take the conversation further and in time you might find the place to talk openly about your differences. For me that has often come when people make a political or theological comment that I disagree with. In some ways they are "checking me out." I need a firmer foundation to know whether I'll be taken seriously if I propose an alternate view, so in the meantime I listen politely so that there might be ground for further conversation. For the moment I suppress my views so that in time there might be an open engagement about the things we might disagree on. Then the conversation will be richer and deeper. It is part of the process to go through this polite stage of the conversation where we all work to develop trust.

Jack

When I first met Jack he put me through the wringer trying to find out if my belief was orthodox in his eyes. Our theological views were a long way apart. I didn't disagree with him or argue with him. With integrity I preached each week. As I preached I made paintings. In each image he saw visually and commented on the fact that the cross was central—which was enough to establish a quality relationship of love and trust that enabled us to talk about living in the deepest places.

ATTENDING AND BEING PRESENT

When you have joined with people, give them your full attention.

Barbara McClintock

In every human endeavor creative response emerges from close attending and observation. Parker Palmer's books have always both affirmed and called something out of me as minister, as teacher, as artist, and as human being. In *The Courage to Teach*, Palmer tells a story about Nobel Prize winning biologist Barbara McClintock. Palmer reports her biographer wanting to know, "What enabled McClintock to see further and deeper into the mysteries of genetics than her colleagues?" McClintock's answer is simple: "Over and over again she tells us one must have the time to look, the patience to 'hear what the material has to say to you,' and the openness to 'let it come to you.' Above all, one must have a 'feeling for the organism'" (Palmer, 1998, 55).

In every field of endeavor the ones who are most creative are the ones who pay closest attention to their material, who see what is there, in acute ways. In conversation it is the same. Conversation that grows creatively requires an alert presence and disciplined observation. Attending means giving yourself fully to the person, the object, the experience before you. It means turning off the interpreting gears and opening your senses to experience the other as fully as possible. It means allowing yourself to experience being with this person.

The stolen car

I went to visit a couple both in their eighties, who had been married fifty-six years. He had been to hospital to have an artery in his head operated on. The medical team decided that he was too old and the operation too risky. It meant that he could have a stroke or die. He said to me, "I know I haven't got much longer to go. A year perhaps?" They were gentle and quiet people. I worked to get them to talk openly about their dying and death. He told me about having their car stolen a couple of times. The second time it was smashed up and he didn't replace it. Such comments sound odd in the circumstance. But attending closely to all that was happening suggested that this man was communicating through a metaphor, a metaphor that said, "Life is being taken from me, just as my car was, and it will not be replaced." It was a way of talking obliquely about his own death when it was too difficult to speak about it directly.

Naming the distraction

If you are attending to someone and suddenly find yourself distracted, a helpful way back into the conversation is to name the distraction. "I'm sorry, I was listening, and when you mentioned your dad I got distracted and was thinking about my dad. Can we backtrack a little?" "I need to tell you that I am a little distracted at the moment. I have just come from a meeting where I became involved in a loud conflict . . ." Once you have named the distraction you can usually let it go and be fully present to the other.

If you have interrupted the conversation to name how you have been distracted it is possible that the conversation might change direction to focus helpfully on your immediate need. It will then be your responsibility to refocus the conversation for the other person: "Thanks for your interest in that. Can we get back to what you were saying?"

LEVELS OF CONVERSATION

When you are attending closely in conversation you will become aware that the conversation changes and it goes to different levels.

Les and Rhonda

Les and Rhonda had recently returned from overseas. In the plan of their life they had decided to teach in a third-world country for three years. On their return the plan was to find jobs and have children. Finding those jobs involved some anguish, but they found them in time. Then they set about having children. Rhonda became pregnant and there was great excitement, joy, and anticipation. Then Rhonda had a miscarriage. Life wasn't so straightforward; it had teeth and the teeth could bite.

I phoned and made a time to visit. I'd visit at 8:30 P.M., after they had got home from work and eaten their evening meal. I went, somewhat awkwardly. I was uncertain as to how I should enter the conversation with them. We sat talking about coffee, houses, and work. Then their big cat climbed on my lap. I don't have a great liking for cats and so ignore them. For some peculiar reason they ignore the people who love them and always claw their way into my lap. And I get very uncomfortable and people notice. So we spent time talking about my discomfort with cats. Slowly we moved into conversation about the government of the day, reflecting together on political decisions and the manner of various state and national leaders. It was a really interesting intellectual conversation. It took about an hour together before we were comfortable about addressing their loss. "I'm really sad to learn about your miscarriage," I ventured. There was some uncertainty in my words and a silence followed. "Tell me what happened."

Slowly we got into talking about what happened. With the story came their emotion, their tears, their anguish, and their grief. Les and Rhonda were sad, heavy, and uncertain. We talked together about their sense of loss: what their hope had been for this child; how their hope had been thwarted. Then we began to talk about the nature of life and creation and God. The created order wasn't perfect, and we were at this moment part of that imperfection. Les and Rhonda were then rethinking their theology and rethinking what they understood about life and about God. It was for them a deep moment when they had to review their lives and, aware in a new way of the risks, plan how they would move ahead. We were in the space of deep prayer whether there were particular words or not. I prayed with them and held their loss and their hope before God.

This conversation had begun slowly, talking about everyday things. Slowly it moved into an intellectual conversation about ideas and government. Then we addressed their loss and the conversation went to another level when emotions were acknowledged and expressed. The conversation went deeper when it reached into the places where life-shaping decisions were made about how to move into the future. Those decisions were accompanied by a rethinking of our worldviews (mine and theirs) as we worked together to understand and name God in this experience. Then from the depths the conversation returned to the ordinary and trivial.

There are four levels in a conversation according to a common wisdom I learned long ago. Conversations begin with "chit-chat"—

such as conversation about the weather or cats and other not too demanding topics. It takes up time and it gives people the chance to feel each other out, to become comfortable with each other. When one moves beyond chit-chat, the movement is to an intellectual conversation, a conversation of ideas, the second level. At this point in its simplest form people begin to have an opinion, for example, about cats. In time those ideas, those thoughts about things become more consequential; they may be thoughts about politics, or thoughts about life.

Some people get stuck talking about ideas because it is safe for them; they are not sure how to talk about emotions. They just keep talking about ideas. If you listen to the stories of people's living you will move people to express their feeling.

This expression of feeling or emotion is a third and deeper level in the conversation. A fourth level of conversation is crisis or life shaping: at this level people are sharing the deep crises of their lives, making life-shaping choices and decisions. This is the level of deep conversation.

To these four levels of conversation I want to add a fifth: the level of the sacred. We enter this level when we recognize the mysterious, the Holy Other, God's voice in the conversation. It is the level of prayer that is beyond words, when you can be present with the other in the silence and know that what is happening is beyond comprehension or description. It is a holy or sacred silence. The discipline of the pastoral person in conversation is to enable and recognize an authentic engagement in this deeper level of conversation and, having recognized it, to be comfortable, to be still, and to be quiet within it. In the conversation with Les and Rhonda, I think we entered this space, and it was shaped, in time, into prayer.

It is important to be aware that conversation goes through these levels to the deeper parts. It does not always reach the deeper levels, nor does it need to. Conversation moves backwards and forwards between the levels. It is important to be aware on which level of the conversation you are engaged and to know how to focus to help the other take the conversation deeper when it is appropriate, and to the "trivial" when that is appropriate.

It is like swimming. You cannot swim to the bottom without first breaking the surface of the water, and after swimming on the bottom you have to swim back from the depth to the surface. Conversation has the same movement.

For practice you could try mapping the movement of a particular recent conversation. Identify the different levels of the conversation, being aware of when the conversation moves to different levels and what happened to facilitate those shifts.

AWARENESS OF THE OTHER

To engage another person in an intentional conversation you have to be aware of the other. It begins with remembering the other's name. This is a really important part of the conversation and a basic affirmation. If you can acknowledge your responsibility for not remembering a name then maybe you can find ways to remember names. If you don't remember a name, it is often because you have made up your mind that you are not going to remember this person's name or because you're not sufficiently interested to be paying close attention when their name is mentioned. See how it might be different if you say, "Tell me your name: it is really important for me to know and use peoples' names." And then you rehearse the name and even some connection that will help you recall it. Remembering and using the other's name is the beginning point for acknowledging an awareness of the other.

When you engage in pastoral conversation it is important to have thought something about who the other is in this conversation. What is their life situation? What is their occupation? What is their economic circumstance? How have they learned about life? What might they teach you about life and faith and God?

You have to be aware that you will have different conversations with different people and that who the other is and that person's experience of life will largely shape the conversation. If you attempt to make every conversation the same, using the same language and metaphor in each situation, you are likely to fail. Listen for the language, imagery, and metaphor of this particular person and use that. When you look at this person—his manner of dress, or the space she is in—or when you hear the stories this person tells, what does it tell you?

Football sweaters

Sunday morning at church in Sydney and three young boys were wearing the shirts of their favorite football team. If I talked with them about their favorite team I was likely to make good connections and soon be able to have a deeper conversation. If I pretended not to see the favorite team shirts I would have been denying an important part of their experience of life. On the other hand if I had gone into the church hall where older people were drinking a cup of tea and had headed straight into a conversation about my favorite football team, it might have been the most absurdly irrelevant thing to say. Have your perceiving antennae about to discern the other before you engage conversation. Being clear about who the other is will help you develop an intimacy with that person.

INTIMACY

Pastoral conversation can have very different ends. Early conversations are often about developing an intimacy where the pastoral person knows the other and the other knows the pastoral person. This is about building a relationship that will be the base for more intimate conversation in the future. Because you have made a relationship on which you can build, sometime in the future you will be in a place to help the other resolve an issue or take the conversation deeper while exploring issues of life and faith.

Facilitating intimacy

Sometimes in pastoral conversation you develop an intimacy that allows a close sharing. Other times your task is to facilitate an intimacy between others. If you are facilitating an intimacy with others your task is not so much to be the "intimate other." Your task is to facilitate an intimacy between people, who already have, and will go on having, an intimate relationship with each other.

When I was young in life and ministry, newly graduated from theological college, I conducted lots of (too many) funerals. Relating with the grieving was something that I felt confident about, for at college I had done a special study on death and grief and I had Granger Westberg's book *Good Grief* (still perhaps the most helpful resource to share with grieving people) under my arm. I am a bit embarrassed to write this now because my practice changed radically later. I'd ring up the chief mourner and find out when he or she would be alone so that I could make a time to visit and listen uninterruptedly to his or her story of grief. When at the end of almost four years I left the parish, I took all those intimate conversations with me. Those with whom I had had the intimate conversations were deserted, the intimacy gone along with me.

Perhaps it was training as a family therapist that helped me realize that the one-to-one, intimate conversation was not the most helpful in this situation. I changed my practice and now ask the widow or widower to invite the whole family (and any others they wanted) to be present at one time. I come at that time to facilitate a conversation between all the members of the family. The conversation is named as preparing for the funeral, as helping the family decide what stories they want to tell about their member who has died. How might the family most appropriately acknowledge and celebrate the life? My task is to enable the family to be intimate with each other, to hear each other's tears, to tell stories in ways that they might laugh and cry together. I ask them to find a story that will tell the essence of this person's life. This is to help the family find its own interpreting narrative.

The end result is, I hope, a relevant and helpful funeral service and a family where all the members are confident to share their anguish and listen to each other. It is a family strengthened by their experience of intimacy and who, by building on that intimate conversation, are enabled to care for each other and participate in their own healing. And I, as pastoral person, could get out of the way and let that happen. (See chapter 19, pages 144–50.)

This awareness that my role is facilitator or coach of the other in the conversation means that I am not seeking in this conversation to create intimate relationships for me, but knowingly and intentionally facilitating the other to work hard on and for their own intimate relationships.

Tina

Tina was a member of my congregation and the mother of a friend. I called to see her and could only stay twenty minutes. The conversation was packed. Tina had high blood pressure and had been instructed by her doctor to rest. "You are in great danger of having a stroke," he had told her. Such information often makes people review their lives, and Tina was no exception. In general terms she was asking, "How do I evaluate and integrate my life?" How do I make sense of this experience called life in the light of the values I have chosen and in the light of my decision to give my allegiance to Jesus?" Even if she did not articulate these questions specifically, that is what I heard her asking in the stories that she was telling.

Tina said, "My mother taught me the faith. If faith isn't practical it is not anything. She talked of her marital relationship, "I've been married fifty-plus years and we are still in love." And "I don't want to boast, but we help people because they are there to be helped." In this short twenty minutes Tina went on telling me about her life, her parents, her spouse, her children, telling me her values and her commitment to them and giving me an assessment of how she felt she had lived according to her values. She told me how prayer had been part of her life and how those around her called and asked her to pray with them.

After I had visited Tina I began to think that I should go back and complete this conversation, allowing a longer time for the conversation to flow. I knew Tina's son well and I knew this was a conversation that he was capable of having with his mother. So I rang and suggested that he have a cup of coffee with me. Over coffee I told him how I could hear his mother evaluating her life. I suggested that this friend continue the conversation with his mother so that the intimacy stayed within the family and the family could be richer for the conversation.

THE COMPETENCE OF THE OTHER PERSON

Recognize, affirm, and address the competencies of the other in the conversation. It is much easier to be in conversation with competent people than incompetent people. If you want people to function better as a result of this conversation an important step will be to acknowledge to them that you see them as competent people and recognize their competence within the conversation. Speak to their competence.

John

John suffered from schizophrenia. Talking with him could be difficult. But by asking him to tell me about his experience of schizophrenia I was asking him to speak from his competence, and the conversation was rich.

Bess

Perhaps similar to valuing someone's competence is valuing that person's reality. Bess was in a nursing home with Alzheimer's disease. I sat with her for a while on one sticky afternoon. She had been tied to her chair so that she couldn't wander. She was distracted, undressing herself. Her shoes were in the trash can. A staff member came into the room and Bess looked at her and said, "I've just been to church." The staff member laughed. I wanted to value Bess' competence so I interpreted: "What she's telling you," I said to the staff member, "is that I'm her minister and that I come from her church." The staff member laughed again. When it came time to go I took Bess by the hand and said "God be with you," and Bess responded "And also with you." As I left, it was, for a moment, as though all the confusion was wiped away. Bess spoke. "Thanks for coming, Doug." So clear was the voice, the sentence, the name, that I was momentarily shocked. Why should I be so shocked, I wondered, if I work to take her reality seriously and to treat her as a competent person? Respecting the reality of the other and treating the person as competent is a complex question when people have Alzheimer's. Bess deteriorated and died a short time later. I like to remember her competence.

TALKING TO PEOPLE'S STRENGTHS

If you value the competence and strength of other people, you will enable more confident speech in them and you will be more able to listen to them.

Knowledge and power

Conversation about theology, baptism, marriage, and lots of other topics can easily weight a conversation towards the knowledge and power of the pastoral person. It's easy. Someone asks to be married in the church. We ask them "Tell me, why do you want to be married in the (or this) church?" or, "What is your understanding of Christian marriage?" The power in such questions lies with the person asking the question because he or she has the "right" information and the ones who want to be married do not. This power differential can be easily and innocently stressed further by asking a couple who want to be married questions that are abstract and difficult to answer. The theologically educated person leading the conversation has read and thought about marriage in an abstract way and so asks, "Tell me how you understand marriage." The couple who has not been married and who has typically not thought theologically about marriage is quickly at a disadvantage and is embarrassed by their powerlessness. In the conversation they fumble to find words that don't come easily.

If the pastoral person asked this couple to talk about their respective parents' marriage they would be empowered to speak of a relationship they have observed and known. Even if the marriage has broken down, and it seems painful for the couple to talk about, it is easier for them to tell stories of their experience observing that marriage than to give idealized opinions about the abstract nature of marriage. Then it is possible to use what they know to help them verbalize the sort of marriage they would like to create.

When people can talk about their own experience in a conversation they are empowered because they are talking about something that they know; the story is their story, the experience is theirs. From that telling of the story of personal experience it is possible to focus reflective thought about the nature of marriage so that each participant in the conversation is empowered.

QUALITY OF LISTENING

Listening well is the guts of what good conversation is all about. It is a basic and crucial part of pastoral conversation. Report back to the other what you hear him or her saying. Tell the other what words you hear. Don't change the words, don't interpret the words, simply ask "Is this what you are saying?" and report what you have heard. Use that person's words.

It is a common and not very helpful practice for people to say, "I hear you" and then go on to say what they want to say. Saying the words "I hear you" does not mean that you have heard the other.

In conversation the only way that you can be confident that you have heard the other is if you report back what you have heard that person say, and he or she in turn affirms, "Yes, that is what I am saying." Don't be shy or embarrassed about this; it is basic to deep conversation.

The bride

I got into conflict with a young couple who wanted to be married. They had put off coming to see me until the very last moment. When they canceled yet another appointment I thought it my duty to raise the tough question: "Are you giving adequate time and energy to preparing for your marriage?" My question was confrontative and caused the bride some distress. She phoned me back and asked if she could come and see me. We met and she told me how "she wanted a minister who wanted to marry them. A minister who would be warm and supportive, caring and interested in them." I said that I wanted to conduct their marriage, that I was pleased to be asked to do it. However, I could not be warm and supportive unless I could also ask the tough questions. For me, their continually putting off coming to see me about the wedding flashed a "red flag." Something was wrong, and I should ask about it. They were busy in their work and other things and those were legitimate reasons for them to put off coming to see me. The bride went on, "We believe we are right for each other. We believe that it is God's will that we marry. We have prayed together about it." Not letting go, I asked why her fiancé had gone inter-state on this day when they had such an important engagement in Sydney. I suggested that the reasons for going inter-state weren't so important that they could not have been postponed a day or two for such an important act as an appointment to organize their wedding. I suggested that patterns like this (that business is more important than the wedding) are the patterns that you carry on after the wedding. "You might find yourself as a young mother at home with small children. You will be alone. You husband will rarely be home, always saying he is too busy at work."

What I want for all marrying people is their happiness. If I genuinely want their happiness, than I am also bound to ask the hard questions in the conversation. The hard questions might cause some pain now and they might prevent the intense pain that comes with marriage breakdown and breakup.

The bride thought that I wasn't hearing her and that mostly I was concerned about my own convenience. I said, "Let me tell you what I can hear you saying and tell me if I'm hearing you accurately or not."

"You have changed the date of your marriage because you want to go on a trip overseas. You want to arrive in Europe in time for a friend's wedding.

You are very busy at work and in the process of selling your business.

You want a special and happy day for your wedding.

You want the wedding at 3 P.M. so that you can go to the beach and take some photographs in the daylight.

You want a minister who wants to marry you.

You think this is an appropriate marriage and you are preparing for it in the right way. You (the bride) have been offended and hurt by my attitude on the phone. You have shown lots of courage by phoning and asking to come and see me today and clear that up."

The bride seemed amazed that I could recall all these things (and more) for her and she began to respond more gently. "You have heard me and I have heard you," she said. I was not sure that she had heard me in a way that was taking me seriously, but it wasn't the time to say that. I summarized what I thought was important: I wanted them to have the best preparation for their marriage. By choosing the minimal legal time there was not adequate time to do that preparation well. In the time that was available I would do the best that I could.

It is difficult work asking tough questions of people in areas where they have much emotional investment. The conversation easily becomes messy. Summarizing the conversation, naming the particular issues for the other can sort through the messes.

Sadly, for me, this couple decided that they did not want me to conduct their wedding and sought the help of another minister. Yet as I mentioned above, I have found that conversations are ongoing. Some years later I met this bride again. The marriage had ended and she apologized to me for not taking my questions seriously at the time. I hurt for the pain of the broken marriage and was moved by the apology.

Using the patterns to shape the conversation

Earlier I mentioned that creative people pay close attention, listen, see, and attend with great discipline. They also look for and see patterns more quickly than others. As you listen, ask yourself: what are the important or recurring patterns in this conversation, in the language and speech of the other, in that person's body language, in allusions made, or in emotions expressed?

You will often find that people come back to the things that are important and repeat them. When you hear a pattern or something that is repeated two, three, or four times, hold up that issue or incident as important. A person might be talking about a relationship and as he or she talks might use the word "intimate" two or three times in a short time. If you are listening well, you could shape a question, "How intimate or close are you feeling with this person at the moment?"

I just want you to listen

Many times you do not have to do any more than listen. People don't want you to solve their problems, think for them, and tell them how to organize their lives. They simply want a listener to be attentive, give them space to speak, and hear them. My wife is inclined to say to me quite appropriately, "I don't want you to solve this, I just want you to listen." What she is saying is that she wants some space to voice what she is thinking and feeling to someone she trusts as an intimate partner. Most people in conversation want such space to speak aloud what they are thinking and feeling, and the knowledge that they will be heard with integrity.

"Nine-eleven"

Often people use shortcuts in their language to describe familiar things. That becomes frustrating when you are listening because you are not sure what they mean. In the United States following the dreadful terrorist attacks on the World Trade Center in New York City and on the Pentagon in Washington, D.C., on September 11, 2001, a shorthand way of referring to these events entered the vocabulary. People began to refer to "Nine-eleven." It was a short-cut way of naming the experience. It was helpful for general communication about the events, and an inadequate way of learning about individual experience on the day. "Nine-eleven" spoke of communal experience. To talk with individuals about what happened for them on that day it is important to ask them to tell the story of their own experience, rather than to assume that the recitation of the words "Nine-eleven" will be adequate. Try asking people "What was your experience of that day?" Everybody has a different story, a different response. Every story is important.

When you hear people using shorthand references to particular events, ask them to tell you their experience of the event. Help them to go slowly and to describe in detail their experience of that time. Short-cut words might also describe character: "He was an utter bastard!" "It's a bit risky for me to ask, but can you tell me in what ways or how he was an utter bastard?"

In conversation often people use short-cut words and they assume that you understand the meaning of those words. And you don't, so you have to ask. It is part of listening.

SHAPING APPROPRIATE QUESTIONS

When you are paying close attention, listening well, and hearing the patterns, you can shape questions that will take the conversation further and deeper. One way to do that is to ask sharply focused questions.

Richard

It was Friday afternoon. I sat in the mall, having coffee with one of my ministerial colleagues. A parishioner of my colleague came along. We invited him to join us for coffee. I quickly learned that Richard's son Tony was dying from AIDS. We had a long and serious conversation about his son, the illness, and what it meant for him as a father.

I asked Richard if he knew some other people from our parish, whose son also had died from AIDS. Richard had been the youth leader when both boys were members of the youth group. He knew that they were different, but at the time he did not understand that they were gay. We talked for a time about this. Richard got up to leave, but I thought there was more to be said. "Richard, I've got one more question to ask you: How could the church have helped you with the issue of your son's homosexuality?" Richard sat down again and our conversation continued intensely for another twenty minutes. Mostly the church could have helped him and his wife by being open about sexuality. Nobody talked about it. It obviously had been a tough, lonely, and confusing time for them as parents battling through the silence of the unspeakable.

This seemed one of those really important pastoral conversations that happens because we were there at the time. The conversation was taken to another level by shaping an important question.

Having asked the question, we needed to give Richard the space to talk. Asking good questions is important. Being willing to listen openly to the response is of equal importance. In the process of the conversation, relax and listen and ask questions that will help the other to keep talking. That can be as simple as asking, "Tell me some more about that . . ."

Where will your questions take you?

Be aware of where your questions will take you. As an artist, when I put a certain mark or color on a painting I have to think through or imagine what will be the effect of putting this mark on the painting before I make the mark. Often many ideas come into my head before I act. I think about each idea, discarding the ones that I don't think workable. Then after significant critical thought I risk the idea that I think will work. Sometimes the idea works, sometimes it doesn't. When it doesn't work I have to find a new way through. The same is true in conversation. You need to think, "Where will this question take the conversation?" Sometimes the question that is in your head will not help the flow of the conversation; no matter how good you think the question, you have to edit it out. And when you consider the direction appropriate (in the light of what you both want from the conversation), then you will ask it.

How and what questions

How you shape your questions will play a significant part in taking the conversation deeper. "How" and "what" questions work better than "why" questions. How questions empower people to consider and act in relation to the conversation.

What happened?

How did this happen?

How will you respond?

What will you do?

How will you survive this?

How will you talk about this with . . . ?

How will you forgive?

These are just some examples. The words you choose and the way you structure your sentences and questions are vitally important. Shaping questions well is crucial because people respond to what you ask them.

THE CONTENT OF THE CONVERSATION

The primary focus of a conversation is "What is this person talking about?" What is the basic thrust or content of his or her speech, what words and images are being used to convey that content, and how is this important for this person in the moment? It sounds so obvious and yet it doesn't always happen. It demands hard concentrated focus on the other, repeating in your own mind what you have heard that person say. It demands putting your own life and agendas to one side in order to give yourself fully to the other.

Setting self aside

I visited a man immediately after his wife had left him. I just went to sit and be present. And of course we talked. As he told me about some of the painful patterns in his marriage I wanted to tell him about how in our marriage we managed those issues differently. It would have been insensitive and inappropriate. So in my head I had to acknowledge things about my own marriage, and let them go while I listened closely to his reality.

In the story at the beginning of this book Bruce speaks in quirky ways. He appreciated when someone took his language and imagery seriously. It is part of the content of the conversation. When you are in conversation use the language of the other. And be aware that by bringing the language of your education or of your particular church or spirituality to the conversation, you can easily exclude the other. This makes the pastoral person more secure and powerful and is often done when the pastoral person is insecure (though he or she might not find it easy to acknowledge that insecurity).

The body

Be aware of the body of the other in conversation. Beyond general posture, try to observe changes in the other's body: changes in breathing patterns—whether people are breathing faster or slower, whether they are breathing deeper or shallower; changes in skin color, particularly around the eyes and the neck; changes in muscle tension in the face, in the hands, in the legs; changes in the tightness in the lips, and so on. The value of this is not to make the pastoral person more powerful by then reporting, "Aha, your lips are tightening or quivering!" or some other clever thing. Rather, being alert to all the cues within the conversation allows you to draw upon that knowledge to be more present, and to take the conversation deeper. It is possible to say, "I am aware that you seem to be close to tears" and leave a silence or to ask the other, "Can you be aware of your breathing for a moment?" Sometimes your observation means you don't speak, you simply honor the silence. Use your observation to help take the conversation into deeper spaces.

Some odd behavior

One day I was having a conversation with a man in my office. He was low in energy, struggling in his marriage and his work. As we talked he reached between his legs and started scratching himself some-where between his testicles and his anus. It was quite odd behavior. His body was telling me something that his words couldn't yet say. I bided my time, and when it seemed appropriate I said, "Tell me about your sex life." He expressed surprise at my question, then went on to tell me in great detail about the struggle he and his wife were having as sexual partners.

Congruence and incongruence

What people say with their mouth and what they are saying with their body doesn't always seem consistent. It is incongruent. When the words and the body and the experience they are describing seem to mesh appropriately we could describe it as congruent. A person might be talking about how they have just been fired from a job they loved. Their words might be pained and their body laughing. You could comment, "It is a bit hard for me to comprehend what is hap-pening. You are telling me this most painful thing and you are laugh-ing." Similarly you might say, "I have difficulty holding the content of what you are saying with the energy that is in your voice."

ANGER AND EMOTION

Being aware of the body of the other can be helpful when people are very angry. That sounds a bit obvious, for when people are angry their bodies give off very scary messages. It is often noticeable from the body first, that people are angry. To respond scared intensifies the conflict. Yelling, arguing, joining the fight won't help. If you can be aware of the other, the anger can be dissipated: stand beside rather than in front of, an angry person, and breathe with them rather than against them. Soon you will find that they will follow your breathing pattern and slow down. Use the language they use. Repeat back to the other person the words you hear them saying. Be in control and slow the words down. Soften the tone of your voice. Be prepared to be still and quiet, giving the other time and space to think, to regain control.

Anger often covers hurt and fear. You can say to an angry person, "Tell me how you are hurting or what you are scared about," and so long as you give the person time and you listen respectfully, he or she will share hurt or fear and move beyond the anger. Don't be in a rush and don't feel you have to control the conversation.

John and Daniel

A former minister in the parish introduced me to a couple who needed some help. Just one month previously their eighteen-year-old son, Daniel, had been killed in a car accident. The family were devastated. The mother's first husband had also died in a car accident. He had spent three years in a coma before finally dying.

My colleague had said there were some "family issues" for this couple. No doubt there were, but how would you find space to talk about them when people are so hurting?

The father, John, was very angry. His anger was focused on the policeman who delivered the message. The mother had said (or at least I heard her say, though she said it wasn't what she intended) that Daniel had talked a week before his death about his death, saying, "and when I die I won't be like Ted (the first husband). I will die in an accident instantly." Then the mother made this statement, "Daniel was stable; you could have thought that Ted might commit suicide." Sometimes, when people die in single car accidents there are questions as to whether the death was accidental or deliberate. As the people were thinking about this, it seemed to me to be important to talk about it. I asked as gently as I could whether they thought Dan might deliberately have taken his life. Quickly they said, "No," and went on to describe the accident in detail. It was a one-car accident in the rain and the car had been wrapped around a pole. I encouraged them to tell the story in some detail.

It is important to have people retell the story of such accidents. When they do, it is emotional and difficult. They will likely cry, experience pain, even be angry. In the telling of the story they are integrating or putting together the pieces of an experience that has ripped them apart. Telling the story allows them to be in control of the experience rather than having the experience, in some suppressed form, control them. Telling the story might also bring the anger to the surface. It did for John.

John was very angry. I had sat with angry people before, so while uncomfortable, I was willing to be present to his anger. My office seemed too small a space to listen to someone who was that angry. I let him express as much of that anger as he was able. Along the way I tried to introduce some rules about expressing anger: "It is okay, and helpful, to express your anger. When you express your anger be safe. Do not use your anger to hurt people, or property, or yourself."

The hurt was too raw and the anger immediate. All his anger was focused on the policeman who brought the message, "Pig! Bastard! I want revenge! I'll make him pay!" The anger rolled on in a vitriolic and irrational way. All I could do was offer a safe place for him to express the anger. I knew that in the circumstance the anger was reasonable. I knew, too, that John had to focus his anger somewhere. He focused it on the policeman. I didn't agree or disagree with him. My task was to listen, to make sure that in expressing his anger, John was safe. On this day, I could offer little more than being willing to hear and absorb the anger.

After such a conversation I needed to find someone to listen to what it had been like for me to hear such anger.

PERMISSION GIVING

To hear and acknowledge the emotion in a conversation takes the conversation deeper. You can also take the conversation to deeper places by giving the other person permission to do and say different things.

People often need someone to give them this permission to do things differently. We all grow up with an odd set of rules in our heads about our living. Sometimes the rules are overt, spoken, and known; other times they are covert and not spoken. These rules, often learned in childhood, control how we function. You can give people permission to let the rules go, to do or say something differently, and to move into deeper spaces. Family loyalty might be the rule. In this family it is inappropriate to criticize any family member. Unspoken is the thought that if you criticize Mum the roof will fall in, the earth open up, disaster will follow. So a daughter holds her hurt at how she was parented too close. Telling her that she's an adult now, and in this safe place it is okay to say how much her mum hurt her, and that such an admission will not be disloyal to her mum, opens the possibility of the conversation going to deeper places.

You will take the conversation deeper by acknowledging that openness is possible in this conversation. People often imagine pastoral people to be religious, pious, tight, controlled, proper, moralistic, and judgmental about what can or can't be talked about, with what words and what emotion. While that unspoken understanding is in place, it is almost impossible to engage someone in good conversation. So somehow you have to break open the possibilities by naming this strange understanding and letting the other person know that this is a space where it is permissible to talk about any subject with any words and any emotion.

You can give people permission to express normally unspeakable thoughts by naming them. I was with a person who I had learned was gambling heavily. How could I address that in gentle way? "You know, when I am struggling and uncertain about life I think about buying a lottery ticket; somehow I think if I win all my problems will go away . . ."

In a similar way you can give people permission to use normally unusable words to express a depth of feeling by introducing those words into the conversation. This is done gently, subtly, and at the right time. "Shit, if that happened to me I would be bloody hurt too!" Sometimes the tight control of language is a symbol of tight control of the experience, the emotion, the worldview, and the religious worldview that prevents God's voice from speaking in fresh ways. Giving people permission to change the language, to find more expressive language is freeing and healing. Sometimes people imagine that their pastoral person will be offended by the "expressive" words that are a normal part of conversation and so they edit them out. It may be easiest for you to say, "I will not be offended if you swear. I would in your situation." If people don't use the full range of their normal vocabulary because of fear of how you will respond it will not be an honest or open conversation. Find ways to help people be comfortable so that they can be fully in the conversation.

Randall

Giving people permission in a pastoral conversation is a lot more than simply saying to someone it is alright to swear. Sometimes people need a different sort of permission. Randall had recently separated from his marriage partner of fifteen years. They had three children. It was a very difficult time for all the members of this family. He was not at all comfortable about the separation. He needed to hear someone say to him that marriage is created for joy, not pain, and sometimes when marriage becomes too painful separation is the only option. There were a lot of messages in his head telling him that he had failed and that he was no good. He felt he should have been in the marriage despite the pain, even though his wife would not negotiate the marriage. Permission giving says to him, in this difficult and painful situation, what you are doing and feeling is appropriate.

At other times, people need specific permission to make moral decisions that might be different from the values they have grown up with or experienced in the dominant culture. Having someone listen with integrity and then say, "Your choice is appropriate," is freeing and affirming.

PACING OR BREATHING THE CONVERSATION

Taking the conversation into deeper places and giving people permission is part of the ebb and flow of conversation. Conversation is like music and it needs to breathe.

Each conversation has a rhythm like breathing. You can be aware that the other needs time to be, to think, and to gather himself or herself. It is easy to be too active in a conversation so that the other is pushed along at such a pace as to not find the conversation helpful. When the conversation doesn't "breathe" people become angry and frustrated and unwilling to be engaged in the future. Breathe the conversation in such a manner that the other person can move in and out in a way and time that is appropriate for that person. This is like the ebb and flow, the breathing in music. What makes music come to life is the space or silence between the notes. Conversation needs the same silences. This breathing of the conversation can be helped by an awareness of the time available for the conversation. If you know how much time you intend to be in conversation then you can pace your questions so that you complete what both people want from the conversation in the available time.

Mavis and Jack

I was in a hospital. Mavis' husband, Jack, had just died and Mavis and I were standing quietly beside Jack's body. How do you say good-bye? What is appropriate? There were a lot of pensive silences. It was a sacred time. A hospital employee blustered in, unaware of our deep prayer. She was doing her job. "Do you want a cup of tea?" Inside me a voice told me to take a deep breath and breathe into the silence, say, "Thank you," then pick up the conversation again, and give it breath and life.

Inevitably there will be times like this when important and intimate conversations are interrupted. Don't get flustered. You can wait for the interruption to pass and then summarize where you thought the conversation was up to, and begin from there. If it is not possible to pick up the conversation, suggest another meeting when the conversation might be continued. If you make the suggestion, be sure that you take the initiative to complete the conversation. Sometimes you will find that the other person chooses that there is no need to continue the conversation. He or she may say that either directly or indirectly by not being able to find the time to complete the conversation. It is alright for the person to pull out. Don't stress yourself about it. Recognize that the person may have resolved the matter, growing from your earlier meeting.

SUMMARY

Strategies like intentionally focusing on what is happening in the conversation and knowing how to attend to the other, shaping good questions, and being open to the expression of emotion will enable you to take conversations deeper. Taking the conversation deeper, breathing it, and valuing the silence moves the conversation toward that which is sacred.

7

THE SPACE OF SACRED CONVERSATION

Let me remind you of something I said earlier, for it is key to understanding the movement into the sacred space of conversation. When caring people engage others deeply in their living, the conversation is pastoral. It is pastoral when they listen to the experience and language of the other. It is pastoral when they listen intensely and without judgment. Sometimes the conversation will go where it seems there are no adequate words. In those instances, the conversation is pastoral when the caring person respects the silences and waits for appropriate images and words to emerge. In these times caring people will find a resonance and reverberation with the stories of faith. In these spaces they will find the voice of God emerging in fresh ways. This is prayer.

STORY AND FAITH IDENTITY

Most simply, when we listen to people tell the story of their lives in a meaningful way we are entering the sacred with them. Recently I had the privilege of being present at two funeral services when different friends told the stories of their mothers' lives in most meaningful ways. What they said was the summation of an intimate, lifelong conversation and, in both cases, because they knew the story of their mothers' lives, they named most appropriately their mothers' souls. When we engage in deep pastoral conversation that names or enables others to name their lives in a meaningful way, we are helping them to name their souls.

When people tell the stories of the significant moments of their lives they will search for metaphors that interpret their experience. As they do so, they are talking about their faith. All people are religious in that they seek to find meaning in their experience; some find the Christian tradition a helpful interpreter of their experience.

Telling stories about our lives could be likened to plaiting a rope. There are many different strands. We tell stories about the family we grew up in, our family in the present, our marriages, our work, and our faith. Then we tell stories about the communities we belong too, the local church, the region, and the nation. We learn history to find the stories that shape national and international identity. When someone has an opportunity to talk about the many strands of a personal life story, that person is naming his or her journey as a faith person. It is as though the person is weaving the strands of the stories into a strong rope that reflects his or her identity as a person of faith.

The sharing of a story in one conversation may be about the upcoming marriage of a family member, and then, in the next conversation, may be reflecting together on an ethical response to a national issue—for example, the effect of unemployment or globalization in the local community. Both conversations, both subjects work to name the faith identity of the participants.

To engage people in telling the stories of their lives and their living is a pastoral act. The telling of stories shapes identity and brings healing and wholeness.

STORY AND HEALING

While the naming of one's life experience or story shapes a knowing of identity and soul, it also works to bring healing following crises. After people have been through distressing events they need to create images that reintegrate what has been pulled apart within them. When a family member dies, or when a marriage ends, or when a person's job is terminated, or when people have a distressing medical diagnosis, and in other similar times people need an opportunity to tell the story of what is happening to them. Often they need to tell the story a number of times. The retelling continues until they have owned and integrated the experience. Such storytelling can be the focus of good conversation. Good care will break the conspiracy of silence that says, "It is time they were over it."

If you know about a distressing event in someone's life you can always ask about it, with sensitivity, and at an appropriate time. If you ask make sure that you can be present to hear the story, "How are you feeling about (that event) now?" Stories often need to be retold and reinterpreted over long periods of time to be healing.

Some people have difficulty telling the story of their lives fully because the experience is very painful and they are scared of the emotion dwelling below the surface. It is important to acknowledge their inability to speak in this situation. Never force a person to speak; instead you can say, "Would this be a good point for us to stop?" That leaves the power with the hurting person to choose in what way they want to continue. "Yes, this would be a good place to stop," or, "Just give me a moment, I need to be able to say this."

Professional help

If you sense that people are stuck in an experience, it might be appropriate to ask if they are getting professional counseling help on this issue. This is the time to recommend a counselor or therapist whom you trust.

Trusted truth-telling

Sometimes your presence allows a trusted truth-telling of the story, which is healing. A father told about the death of his son, whose photograph was on the mantelpiece. "I tell people that he died in an accident. It is easier. The truth is that he took his own life." The conversation flowed into telling the story of both men's lives in a meaningful way.

VALUING THE SILENCE

Sometimes the stories heard or the circumstances in which you meet someone lead into silence.

Silent conversation

To move into the sacred space of conversation you will need to value silence. A couple of the most significant conversations of my life were with my dad following two significant operations, one for a brain tumor and the other for bowel cancer. Both conversations included long times of silence when I sat beside his bed. Sometimes I read, sometimes I drew, and sometimes I used the silence to meditate, pray, think, and plan. And for good periods of time I thought about the life we had shared and in the silence I thanked him for the gift of the shared journeying.

Conversation can involve periods of silence when you are present with another and no words are spoken. No words are necessary, or appropriate; they are not required. When there are no words, to try and make words happen ruins the moment.

Some people find it difficult to be in a conversation where people don't speak. If you can learn to value silence as an important part of the conversation you will find it easier to be present when longer periods of silence come. Breathe quietly and deeply; attend to and hear your body in the silence. Take the opportunity in the quiet to review where the conversation has come and is going. Use your eyes to listen for a while. Look at the other person and be aware of what is happening to and for them. Respect that person's need to be silent. Often silence comes at times of deep emotion and intense awareness. By being silent you are valuing the intensity of the deep moment. When you respect the silence good things happen in the conversation.

THE CHAOTIC SPACE OF NOT KNOWING: TOUCHING THE SACRED

Silence can be peaceful, but it can also heighten a sense of chaos. In so many of the conversations reported in this book there was a time when I didn't know what was happening or what to do. When Bruce (in the opening story) sat telling me about his experiences in a prisoner of war camp when he had just learned that his wife would die, I didn't know what was going on; it seemed chaotic. From the chaos of not knowing I discovered that something sacred was happening. Through metaphor Bruce was naming a deep part of his faith, a part that would sustain him in the desert of grief ahead.

In many conversations you will enter the chaotic space of not knowing what is happening. You don't know what will happen next, and you do not know how to continue the conversation. It feels like you have lost control. You are uncertain about what is happening inside yourself, you do not know if you have resources to be this deeply involved, and you do not know if there is a way through. This sensation is chaotic. It is easy to do something that will put you back in control, but this something won't allow the new possibilities for the other. When you don't know, when it feels chaotic, be still, be quiet, and allow the other space and time. That person will find a way forward. If it is difficult to be still and quiet, name the chaos, name all that you don't know, and then, be still and quiet.

The creative space, the space of the imagination, the space for the voice of God in pastoral conversation is so often the space of chaos. In the biblical narratives creation comes from chaos, water comes in wilderness, flowers bloom in the desert, light comes in darkness, resurrection comes in death. Wilderness, desert, darkness, and death are all places of chaos and they are the places where the voice of God is heard afresh, as new and life giving. A willingness to enter the conversational space of chaos with the other is a willingness to make the conversation sacred.

It is possible through practice and reflection to increase your ability to sit quietly in the midst of chaos. The discipline of the silent retreat enables the retreatant to move into the space of chaos and darkness and discover within it the voice of God. It is formational for pastoral ministry. It equips the pastoral person to enter, to listen, and to find voice in the chaos and darkness of the lives encountered in pastoral conversation.

An ability to engage the conversation to the point that you enter this place of chaos distinguishes this as pastoral conversation. In like manner, a disciplined openness to that which emerges in the chaos, the ability to discern the images and voices that are of God and to offer that which leads to healing, wholeness, justice, and hope, distinguishes this as pastoral conversation. It transforms the conversation from the ordinary into the sacred.

BEING A THEOLOGICAL INTERPRETER IN THE CONVERSATION

The one who can identify and name the sacred nature of the conversation becomes a theological interpreter. That person brings to conversation a knowledge of the Christian tradition and an ability to identify and name in the conversation that which is of God. The conversation will be qualitatively different for this awareness. Without discipline it is easy to slide into glib pious response. With discipline it is possible to offer profound wisdom. Following the tragic death of a niece, the minister of our church came to visit. He was present to us, listened deeply, and didn't try to offer cheap consolation or pious words. A day later he returned with a poem he had written that reflected something of the desolation we felt as we stood bereft before God.

The mother of a teenage daughter

Pastoral people stand and are formed in the Christian tradition, and, they attend to other's experience in the present. Imagine a conversation between yourself as pastoral person and the mother of a seventeen-year-old girl who finds herself pregnant and contemplating a termination. There are no easy answers. No glibly quoted texts will help. You stand together as people formed in the Christian tradition, listening hard to one another. The mother wants help to care for her daughter and to know how to move on. The only option is to be still and listen in the silence. You may want to go away and read and think and become more informed. Ultimately you have to fill in the space that exists between your experience as a Christian person and this other Christian person's experience. To fill that space requires an act of the imagination when together you listen for the images that form and then listen for how those images speak to the present situation. Together you listen to find an ethic of care and justice. This is theological reflection. This is listening for the voice of God in the present. Its very uncertainty makes it tough work.

Inevitably this will lead to how we name and mark conversation as sacred.

SUMMARY

When you listen to the stories other people tell of their experiences of living, when you help them tell those stories in ways that give meaning to their lives, you are talking about their souls. When you help people tell stories of the painful and discordant events of life, you are shaping healing. When you walk with people into the spaces of silence and/or chaos, you are walking into the space into which the voice of God breaks in fresh ways. When you are alert as a theological interpreter, you can enable people to hear the voice of God anew.

THE PASTORAL PERSON IN THE CONVERSATION

SHARING YOURSELF

You are a presence in a conversation. You are there with your body, your senses, your mind, and your speech. Be open to sharing yourself without allowing your needs to take over the conversation. Pastoral conversation reflects that we are community in which we share deeply about our living. When we share of ourselves, we are acknowledging and sharing our common humanity under God. Sharing yourself will make the conversation more equal. It will be less unidirectional if both participants are able to share something of their lives. The pastoral person can share significant life issues, experiences, questions that affirm the other in the conversation, being careful that any such sharing doesn't take over the conversation. Giving of self goes two ways in good conversation, so just as we need to be willing to receive and acknowledge the gift of the other, we should also give appropriately of our selves.

Receiving the Gift of the Other

When we share ourselves in conversation we come away energized because what we have been able to give has been received as important and valued. In a reciprocal way when we receive the gift of the other we allow that one to feel important and valued. To decline or refuse to accept this gift is to deny that person some possibility of being empowered in the conversation.

Vi

When we visit a home the host offers a drink and we accept the hospitality. In some cultural settings not to do so could cause affront. Some people offer other gifts. Vi was ninety and knew that she was getting to the end of her life. She had few people with whom to share her resources. Whenever I visited, she always had a huge bag of candy waiting as a gift for my children. Should I accept the candy or not? It seemed important to receive the gift because it valued and empowered Vi. I was clear in my mind that I was not visiting in order to get the sweets. If I got too worried about her gifts it would have made difficult my ability to be a conversation partner. Her ability to give me something and my ability to receive it valued who she was.

Vi's giving of candy was her way of touching me. Physical touch was important for Vi too. She always reached out and touched me when I came to visit and when I left.

TOUCH

Touching and being touched is an important part of being human. Jesus recognized this in his ministry. As part of his conversation, he touched people in ways that brought healing. After a sudden death, when no words are ever adequate, taking someone in your arms and holding them might be the most appropriate way to speak.

Touch has always been an important part of conversation and will remain so. Holding a hand in a hospital room, touching someone on the shoulders or arms as a way of acknowledging or affirming, making the sign of the cross on the forehead or a hand, responding to a request for a hug, or greeting with a kiss can all be appropriate ways of acknowledging that people need to be touched and that touch heals. Ashley Montagu's classic book *Touching* is a helpful resource in thinking about the role and place of touch in care.

Yet touch is intimate. When we are intimate we need to establish clear and appropriate boundaries.

SETTING CLEAR BOUNDARIES

Pastoral conversation is also intimate and we need to set clear boundaries. Setting boundaries can have a number of functions. Good boundaries can protect you from getting too involved when you don't need to be. They can be used to help the other people solve their own problems. And they are important in establishing healthy and appropriate relationships in community.

Ross and Liz

Ross rang me in great distress. He and Liz lived in the local community, and their teenage children came to our church youth group. He told me they had had a "vituperative" conversation with their sixteen-year-old before he stormed out of the house. "Could you help?" At the time I was exhausted, and the thought of helping them drained all my energy. Inside I felt like I had nothing to offer. I suggested to Ross that it might be helpful for them to see a family therapist and recommended someone whom I trusted. Then I said, "Don't chase your son. Let him go. Trust that he will survive. Plan how you can survive this time. Sit and wait. I will call in tomorrow just to say hello."

To survive I needed to set a boundary and I did. It might seem like the boundary was for my convenience, and at one level it was, for I was very tired. At another level my setting a boundary about what I was willing to do would empower the family. Problems like this one don't just happen; they have been building for a long time. My running to be with this family would not change anything. Helping them to allow their sixteen-year-old some space and time was a good and positive thing to do. It would allow him to move toward adulthood by accepting responsibility for his life and being, and it would allow Ross and Liz to let go, just a little bit, of their maturing son. All three would get some time to cool down emotionally. I could join the conversation in a slower and gentler way after the family had resolved the crisis. As a result this family would be more powerful and functioning in a healthier way.

Sometimes I need to set a boundary because I don't want to be involved in a conversation. Perhaps the time isn't appropriate, perhaps I'm uncertain about where the conversation will go, or maybe I think I'm going to be used.

A late-night private talk

We lived in a house that was very public. One night at 11:00 P.M. a young man came to the back door. He seemed a bit spaced out, probably on drugs. He wanted "the Father." He had a problem and asked, "Can we go somewhere private and talk?" My breathing became shallow, my anxiety high. I did not want to be in a conversation where I had to say a clear "no" to a manipulative request for help, late at night. The young man walked across to our garden furniture and sat down. I stood, and by so doing, was saying that I was going to be clearly in control of this conversation. "My bank card bill is due tomorrow for $4,500 and I've got to pay them $45." I didn't listen for too long before I interrupted and told him to come back to the community aid organization across the road at 9:00 the next morning and ask to see the financial counselor. He got up and left without any further words. I went inside disturbed and unable to sleep.

It is impossible to answer every request for help. It is appropriate sometimes to say, "No" and to set clear boundaries, even though sometimes setting those boundaries is disturbing. Knowing how to say, "No" in this setting will help me know how to say, "No" when I might be becoming too intimate.

Deep conversation is intimate and people in pastoral conversation are vulnerable to the possibility of being inappropriately intimate. In close conversation there is a continuum of words, emotions, being taken seriously, being heard deeply, that can easily move into touching, sexual intimacy, and sexual expression. Be aware that when you spend time with people and listen to them it can be sexually stimulating. Know your limits. Remember that this is a pastoral relationship. Set clear boundaries. Be safe.

Knowing my own boundaries, knowing in which relationships I meet which needs is important self-awareness. Because I am in what I perceive to be a good and intimate sexual relationship, it is easy for me to say that I meet my needs for intimacy and my needs for sexual expression in my marital relationship. It is much more difficult for those who are single, or those whose intimate relationships are under pressure and where sexual needs are not met in a fulfilling way. *Even so*, those who enter pastoral conversation need to be aware of where and how they meet their need for intimacy. In conversation they must set clear and specific boundaries.

In this regard, think about what guidelines and practices you use and communicate to ensure that unambiguous boundaries are set and known in your pastoral relationships. How do you typically say to another person, "I am not comfortable with this level of intimacy at this place and time. I wonder if we might meet at the coffee shop, in the parish hall (etc.)? I would feel safer talking with you there."

It is likewise important to acknowledge and name how you as a pastoral person intentionally foster, nourish, and live those relationships that meet your needs for intimacy. I was away from home and involved in leading a weekend program. A woman flirted with me, giving very loud messages about her sexual availability. I responded by saying, "I'm married. I value the sexual relationship I have with my wife as a unique expression of our intimacy." I was clear, and I was heard.

Though there are some "grey areas," let me suggest what is appropriate and what is not appropriate as expressions of intimacy in pastoral conversation:

- Hold your conversations in places that are safe for both of you. That might mean being where you can be seen by others.
- Know your boundaries. Be willing to name them when necessary.
- Phone ahead to make appointments rather than randomly drop in to visit people.
- When you visit, choose appropriate times.
- Limit your touching of the other person. This is one of the "grey" areas, since the Christian tradition recognizes healing through the laying on of hands. Touch is important, but it must be appropriate.
- Be wary when you find you are having conversation with someone because "they need you," or because "you need them."
- Be wary both when you find that you don't want them to go, and when you find yourself seeking someone out without really knowing why.
- Reflect on all your conversations and be able to name with integrity what needs of your own you are meeting in the conversation.
- Be wary of your thinking or fantasizing of the other person as a sexual partner.

Pastoral conversation is intimate. Be vulnerable, be safe, know your role and your place, and set appropriate boundaries.

9

CONCLUDING THE CONVERSATION

When I am teaching I know that the class will come to an end at a certain time, and I plan my class with that time in mind, bringing it to an appropriate end. The abstract paintings that I make, on the other hand, take months and months because I don't have an idea of what the work will be like. It unfolds and reveals itself slowly. Over the long term conversation can be like that. Particular conversation is like teaching: you have an end point in mind and you work to bring it to an appropriate end. Sometimes conversations drift on interminably because those who participate in them don't know how to conclude the conversation.

To bring the particular conversation to an appropriate close, begin by focusing the conversation, clarifying the agenda, and being aware of what questions will help get to an appropriate resolution. Be aware of, ask, clarify what the other person wants from the conversation and be clear about your expectations. If you have a time limit, say so, for then you can work to a plan, and by doing this you can then acknowledge when that has been achieved. At the conclusion of a conversation it is appropriate to summarize where the conversation has gone and what has emerged from it. As you bring the conversation to completion, think about how you can mark it as an important conversation.

In finishing a conversation make sure that people feel valued and affirmed as a result of being in the conversation. Think how you feel at the end of a good conversation where the other person has acknowledged and affirmed you. You can gift the other by making that person know that he or she is important to you. In the section on quality of listening I told of getting into conflict with a young couple who wanted to be married. After summarizing what I had heard the woman say I affirmed her strength in coming to see me, "You have shown lots of courage by phoning and asking to come and see me today to clear the matter up." I did not just make this up so that she would feel good. The affirmation had to be true. It had taken a lot of courage to phone back and ask to see me.

MARKING THE CONVERSATION

How might we celebrate or mark pastoral conversation? Sometimes the celebration is in a hug. The significance of a conversation may also be marked by gentle touch, naming that the conversation has been important, or by the reading of a psalm, or the sharing of prayer. The celebration or marking needs to be negotiated. "Would it be appropriate for me to give you a hug?" "Would it be appropriate for me to pray with you?" Such an invitation allows the other room to say either "Yes, please" or "No, thank you." You might finish a conversation simply by saying "God be with you."

Hal

I went to see a friend, Hal, who was in a crisis. I was with him for an hour and a half. The conversation was emotional and meandering, more about being present than anything else. He took a couple of phone calls and I sat quietly. When I got up to leave Hal asked if he could have a hug. We wrapped our arms around each other and stood quietly for maybe ten seconds. He said, "Thank you for not offering to pray." The conversation was more than an ordinary conversation and he wanted to mark that in some way. It came in the hug. I guess that his thanking me for not praying was that I related to him as a friend and not as an "object of ministry." The hug was how friends mark closely shared experience.

With Hal it wasn't appropriate to pray. Discerning the appropriate time and place for prayer requires a perceptiveness to the need, circumstance, and worldview of the other. Sometimes it isn't appropriate to pray and the pastoral person has to discern that, and at the same time be open to where the conversation might go, what the focus of the conversation might be, and how the conversation might be intentionally pastoral.

I am aware that some pastors choose to complete every conversation with a prayer. I find the experience very intimate and cannot offer prayer all the time. Discerning the appropriate moment requires an open sensitivity to the other. Knowing when not to pray is as important as knowing when to pray.

Monty

Even at the time of death, some people want a minister and not prayer.

I conducted the funeral for Monty, whom I had neither known nor met. The four people who sat in the front seat of the crematorium chapel were likewise unfamiliar to me. Standing in front of them, I asked them to tell me about their friend. One of the four friends was Monty's social worker, and she responded by reading from a piece of paper in which Monty described himself as an agnostic. Another of the friends had brought a poem to read. I emphasized to this small group that we had come to acknowledge Monty's life, and yet the service would be for us who had gathered. "What would help us now to name and acknowledge his life?" None of the people wanted prayer, they were not sure how a psalm would help, and they didn't want the word "God" to be used. So I made a time of silence and said, "Be thankful for Monty and be thankful for his life." I left some minutes of silence, judging what I thought appropriate in the circumstance. Then I walked over to the coffin, put my hand on it and committed the body to be cremated, "in the hope that the mystery of life will be answered for Monty at this time." I concluded the service by saying, "Peace be with you, the friends of Monty, who have come to acknowledge his life." I didn't want to put words or a style of language on the people that they did not want. Something in me finds it difficult to lead a funeral service without words of hope. At the end, the gathered friends suggested it would be appropriate to play Beethoven, for "Monty loved Beethoven." Sadly, we didn't have any Beethoven to play.

In this setting I think I marked the conversation as pastoral, and made space for prayer in a way that respected what the people wanted. In this circumstance Beethoven would surely have been prayer.

APPROPRIATE PASTORAL PRAYER

Beethoven would have been prayer at Monty's funeral, because the music would have taken us into the space that is beyond speech, the space where our deepest yearnings are held before God. That begs a question: What is it that shapes appropriate pastoral prayer? I have always been scared of piety and want a pastoral prayer to be a genuine and simple holding of the life of the other before God. Pastoral prayer uses the resources of faith, particularly the prayerful voice of the pastoral person, to hold another before God. A simple structure is: to thank God for the life given to us, to thank God for the ones with whom that life is shared, and then in one or two brief sentences to hold, as if on open palms towards God, the concern and celebrations of the one(s) with whom you have been in conversation. As simply as possible, name the other(s) before God.

Jean

I went to the hospital to visit Jean, who was dying. Her sister, Nell, and her adult children, James and Sheila, were with her. Leaning over the bed, I quietly told Jean who I was. I listened for just a moment, and then said, "Are you are ready to let go?" "Yes," she said, "but I can't see the door yet." I sat quietly with that. I was aware of an amazing intimacy in the statement. I asked Jean, "Are there any things in life that you want to do before you go through the door?" "No," she said, "and I'm not scared of going through the door." I said to her, "It is appropriate to be ready, to have lived life in its fullness, and to be ready to go through the door." She said, "My family, my life have been wonderful."

The family who had been present when I came in left me alone with their mother. I talked a little more with Jean. She seemed very tired, so I offered, "You seem to be tired, could I pray with you and then leave you to sleep?" "Please do," she responded.

I prayed, thanking God for life, for those with whom Jean had shared life. I asked that God would show Jean the door, be present with her as she passed through the door, and give her and her children peace. It might have been more appropriate to share this prayer with the sister and adult children, but they left me to be alone with their mother, and it seemed appropriate that I pray just with Jean. I didn't have to repeat all that we had said. God had been present with us. Now I wanted Jean to know that we were holding her and this next stage of her life before God. I used her language, her metaphor of the door as a way of affirming her reality. God would hear far more than the few meager words I spoke.

By trusting that God has been present and has heard the whole conversation, you don't have to repeat all that has been said. The

83

deep open pastoral conversation is itself prayer; this small ritual at the conclusion acknowledges the sacredness of the sharing that has occurred.

I will never cease to be amazed at the importance of such prayer for people. Oftentimes I have looked up after the prayer to see the tears of the other roll down their cheeks. Sometimes people responded by praying for me too. I have always been grateful for those gifts.

SUMMARY

To bring the conversation to a close, know what you both want from the conversation. When you think that has been achieved, summarize what has been spoken of. Mark the conversation in a way that names its importance. If appropriate, pray for the other.

AFTER THE CONVERSATION

YOU ARE ON HOLY GROUND

Praying with someone is a very intimate activity for me, and I do not do it easily or lightly. It makes me think that the privilege of engaging in deep conversation about people's living is something very sacred and needs to be treated that way. Your privilege is to be invited into intimate spaces. Much is made of the notion of confidentiality in conversation. Being confidential has become a "rule" and with it has come a secretive, and to my mind, unhealthy rigidity. Conversation involves at least two people. If you genuinely engage conversation you will be impacted, changed, converted. It is difficult not to talk about your experience as a result of the conversation. This doesn't mean gossip. It doesn't mean that you have to tell the details of another's life in order to integrate your own. At the beginning of the second chapter I told a story about Grace, how I went to her flat and she told me that her children had kept from her the knowledge of her former husband's illness and death. I learned so much from that conversation that has shaped my worldview. Now I cannot name my valuing of long-term commitment in marriage as a higher value than genital faithfulness or my understanding of forgiveness without telling this story. It is sacred ground for me because of what I learned in the conversation. At the same time I respect and value how important the conversation was for Grace.

In Exodus the story is told of Moses' encounter with the voice of God coming from a bush that was burning but not being consumed.

The voice of God said to Moses, "Take off your shoes; you are on holy ground." When you enter pastoral conversation do so respecting that it is holy ground. Take off your shoes. Treat the experience of the other, treat what you hear, as sacred: take off your shoes, for you are indeed on holy ground.

REFLECT AND REMAIN ACCOUNTABLE

Taking off your shoes because you are on holy ground is a wonderful metaphor. How might you do that? A place to begin is to reflect on and be accountable for the conversations you have.

The christening

I went to visit a young couple in their home and to talk with them about having their child baptized. They had been married in our church, and now that they had a child they wanted that child "christened." "Never been to church, well, not since I was eight or nine," the father said. I got the impression they didn't have any desire to go again, that for them, the christening would be a ceremony to ritually celebrate the wonderful gift of the birth of their child. I attempted some education by telling them, "We use the term baptism, not christening. It is a ritual to mark the inclusion of your child into the Christian community. It claims the child as one of Jesus' people to represent him in the world. It is an act of God's grace that God accepts our children in baptism." I mentioned the confusion in the culture where people appropriately want a ritual to mark and celebrate birth, and the failure of the general culture to offer such a ritual. I invited this young couple to come to church before the baptism day, "to get a feel of the place, to know what goes on, to let the community know you."

There was something uncomfortable in this conversation. I was talking and they were talking, but we didn't seem to be connecting. After half an hour I left. This couple's life and marriage seemed to be totally dominated by their first child. Aware that it is easy for people to make child-centered families that create problems later in the leaving-home stage of the family life cycle, I offered a little advice: "Look after your marriage; go out without your child; use your parents as babysitters. If you have a happy marriage you will have a happy child," and more similar advice. What I was saying seemed not to be connecting with them, so I left. He followed me down the stairs calling after me, "What's your name? I'm not good on names, always forget names. Write down for us your phone number, just in case we need to ask you something."

How can I be accountable for my role in a conversation like this? It is not helpful to blame them, saying they didn't really understand baptism. How could I learn from this conversation so that in subsequent conversations I could do it better? The conversation made me think hard about the nature of their request and the nature of baptism.

Reflecting later in my journal, I wrote about how I struggle with the issue of baptism when people come from outside the church. I see the conversation about baptism as offering a stepping stone, a way to invite people to trust the grace of God in the act of baptism. Over time, I also have come to understand that the experience of the birth of a new child makes people feel at one with God the creator. They want with all their being to acknowledge that connection. The difficulty is that they do not have an adequate language to express it, so they simply ask that we (the Church) baptize their child. Can the symbol of baptism work on its own, or do the parents have to have some sense of what the baptism means?

Is it enough to write this in my journal or do I have to be more accountable to others in my reflection on conversation?

My journal

Writing in my journal has been a helpful discipline over many years. Each morning, as I begin the day, I take time to reflect on the experiences of the previous day. I write about those conversations that engaged me deeply and reflect on them, listening to myself with the same discipline that I listened to the other in order that I might learn about myself and how I function in conversation in hopes of improving. My journal writing has become an important part of my prayer discipline. In this way I am opening my pastoral function before God. I am praying for the people given to my care and praying for myself in the pastoral role. With discipline, I hope that I am open to God.

Other ways of being accountable

Beyond the journal you can give an account of, and get support for, your participation in conversation by using a supervisor, spiritual director, or support group. Such structure is important if we are to be effective in conversation.

In the parish setting I found it helpful to have a pastoral support group where I reflected openly with others on my role, function, and dysfunction in pastoral conversation. I wanted to show that I was accountable for how I went about my task as pastor. I felt that if I could talk openly with them about my ministry perhaps they would recognize that we are equals in ministry. In addition, perhaps I could model reflective practice as a discipline for shaping engaging pastoral conversation. Always such group time ended with the responsive or collective reading of a psalm. From the outset I modeled what the group could be by opening my own practice to thoughtful comment by others. It was my responsibility to make sure that we kept the focus on being accountable for and learning from pastoral encounters.

LIFELONG LEARNING

Being accountable for how we share in pastoral conversation means that we will continue to develop our competence. Being competent in pastoral conversation is a lifelong task. That is why I hope that you might come back to this text regularly so that you keep reflecting, you keep thinking, and you keep learning in ways that will enrich your pastoral engagements, and together you might listen afresh to the renewing voice of God.

BEING OPEN TO CONVERSION

An openness to your own conversion as a result of pastoral conversation opens you to your own growing edges.

Tom and Barbara

I hadn't really formed my views on homosexuality until I met Tom and Barbara, whose son Stephen was dying from AIDS. I'd thought about it as more or less an abstract issue. As I sat with Tom and Barbara and heard the story of their journey with Stephen, I had to rethink. The conversation was not some hypothetical "out there" discussion. It was Mum and Dad reflecting on their child's journey from birth. They reflected on how he was different and how there wasn't a choice to be gay. He lived who he was, as one made in the image of God. Now his parents wept for a life destroyed by disease. What does it mean for parents that they bury their child? The tears burning the faces of Tom and Barbara pushed me to think in new ways. Most simply, my worldview changed. With my awareness of what this family

went through I became aware of many more families in the community with gay children. This was demanding conversation because I
had to change as a result of being in it.

Being open to conversion in a conversation is demanding. To give
myself fully and openly to the other person has demanded that I rethink what is important in life. Pastoral conversation is never about
abstract ideas; it is always about lived lives. When you have conversations with people who have major ethical decisions to make, you
have to be open to the new possibilities for yourself that result from
the conversation. Meeting people with tough ethical decisions to
make in the workplace, those who want to change the world politi-
cally and socially, those who want to bring about justice or heal the
earth or serve in ministry—all such encounters open you to seeing life
differently. Being in conversation with someone whose marriage is so
painful that to stay in it would be to destroy lives, or with a young
unmarried woman who wants to talk about the pregnancy termination she has had, also opens us to see the world differently. These conversations change both participants.

"Hans Georg Gadamer . . . reminded us that only those who are
willing to put their presumptions at risk can engage in true conversation. We may not change our minds, but we cannot have genuinely
confronted otherness and remain utterly the same; and we don't
know ahead of time what the difference might be. . . . true conversation always puts conversants at risk, because you cannot truly converse without risk of conversion." (Cowan and Lee, 1997, 2–3)

When pastoral people engage in conversation while closed to the
possibility of their own conversion, the other person in the conversation will know and hold back. Equally, if the other participants sense
that the pastoral person is open to conversion, they too will be open
to conversion.

PASTORAL CONVERSATION IS DEMANDING

People who have engaged in serious conversation often report how
tired they are afterwards. Indeed, it is intellectually and emotionally
demanding to be genuinely present to the other in conversation; it
demands a lot of energy.

This energy drain or anxiety often begins when the pastoral carer
is preparing for the visit or conversation. Even though you may have
phoned and made an appointment and so can assume you are ex-

pected, walking to the door of the one you will visit can be an uncertain and anxious time. "What will I say? How long should I stay? What if I am bored? Will I be able to listen? What will they think of me?" and numerous other questions rush through the mind.

Being in intensely focused conversation requires disciplined concentration and that is tiring. Similarly when conversation is emotional or addresses life crises, your ability to give yourself to the other is exhausting. You come away tired.

Andrew and Jan

Having learned that Andrew's younger brother Clive was critically ill, I went to visit Andrew and Jan. The hour and a half I spent with them seemed like much longer. Andrew told the story so slowly, so deliberately, so fairly, and it was deep, emotional, and frightening. I asked questions like, "What happens for you, Andrew, when you see your brother like this?" I was aware that Andrew and Clive's mum had died in their childhood and I wondered about the shadow of that experience on this experience. So, as a way of bringing that shadow into the open, I asked how old the boys were when their mother died, and how this illness reminded Andrew of his mum. I asked how Andrew's dad was functioning through this time.

Then I prayed with Andrew and Jan. They were both in tears and deep silence at the end of the prayer. "Thanks for coming." Andrew said.

The visit was very hard, exhausting work. It was the end of the day and I was very tired. It demanded something extra of me to move into their space, and to listen. This is for many the invisible part of the church's life: the close pastoral conversations in life's major crises. While demanding and exhausting, such encounters are also great gifts. It is amazingly rewarding and energizing to be invited into the intimate moments of people's lives.

Demanding and energizing

Conversations can be both tiring and energizing at the same time. While giving your attention fully to the other is tiring, being allowed into the deep and intimate places of another's life is an energizing privilege.

It is helpful to think about what activities give you energy and what activities take away your energy. Regular physical exercise gives me energy, as does going to art galleries, being with my wife, conversation with good friends, and painting. Other things take or drain my energy. In order to be able to engage the demands of close conversation I have to build into my life regular activities that give me energy.

SUMMARY

Be aware that you are on holy ground when you engage people in conversation. Respect the sacredness of that which is shared with you. Take the time to reflect on and learn from your conversations. Use a journal. Be a lifelong learner. Be open to conversion. Know that pastoral conversation can be demanding and so build into your life practices that renew your energy.

Part Two

CONVERSATION IN SPECIFIC PASTORAL SITUATIONS

PREPARATION AND PRACTICE

What can you do in specific situations? How do you know what to say when you first meet someone? What can you talk about if you visit after the birth of a baby? How do you have a conversation in the workplace? How do you talk about faith? This chapter and those that follow suggest strategies for engaging in particular conversations. They offer suggestions that might inform particular conversations.

PREPARING BY NAMING YOUR OWN LIFE STORY

If you want to improve your conversational ability, a starting point is to attend to and tell your own life story. We all want and need our own lives to be heard. Taking the time to tell the story of your own life in a journal and then to another person is good preparation for conversation not least because it frees you to be present to the other.

Spend significant time exploring and naming the story of your life. Use the questions that are scattered through this section of the book. For example, if you are reading the section on conversations with people preparing to be married, or the section on conversations with people about faith and life, choose some of these questions to focus your own reflection. In a quality book write about the important moments, include photographs and drawings, interview important people about key events.

PRACTICING PASTORAL CONVERSATION

Alongside of exploring your own story, practice pastoral conversation. Interview a friend about a particular experience in his or her life, such as birth, death, marriage, divorce, separation, job loss, injury, achievement, celebration, or life transition. At the conclusion of the conversation you might ask for some feedback: How well did you listen? Were your questions helpful? What did your body language say in the conversation? Did you give the other adequate time?

In preparation for the conversation think about the following things. They have been addressed in various ways in the previous section of the book:

- What is the intent/purpose of the conversation for you and for the other person? (Both people in the conversation will have expectations about the conversation and it is important to clarify both sets of expectations. If you do not clarify expectations you are often talking at cross-purposes.)

- How will you be present to the other person?

- What will help that for you, for the other person ? What will hinder that for you, for the other?

- What questions will be important to ask for yourself? And for the other?

- What other information about you and about the other person will shape your questions? (What is the other's gender, age, stage in the life cycle, relational history, interest, need, and so on?)

- How will you shape your questions? (Remember that "how" questions will take you further than "why" questions. Asking people to tell you about an experience will offer an open-ended way to enter the conversation.)

- Where will your questions take you? Where will your questions take the other?

- How and when will you bring the conversation to a conclusion?

- What will distinguish this as pastoral conversation?

- How will you celebrate or mark the conversation?

If having a conversation with someone about a specific event like birth, marriage, separation, or death in the family, the following guidelines might be helpful in finding out how they perceived the event or experience:

- What is it that you want to come from this conversation for you, and for them?
- As you ask the questions remember that you, as pastoral carer, will need to give your attention as the other tells of his or her experience.
- Name the particular experience (for example, birth, marriage, separation, death) that you want to focus on. Say why you want to focus the conversation this way. "I'm working to develop some skills in pastoral conversation. Would you be willing to have a coffee with me when we might talk together about your experience of the birth of your child (or other, as appropriate)?"

The following questions help to get another person into the "flow" of a story. The more of these details you can ask others, the more likely they are to touch their memories and reflect more deeply on the experiences. Remember this is a "practice" so try it and see. You will find a flow within the conversation and when you do you may find that too many questions inhibit rather than help the conversation. Go slowly. Don't rescue the other person by answering for him or her and, at the same time, work to keep the flow alive.

Ask the other person to describe in as much detail as possible the experience, event, or transition.

- What do you recall of the day?
- What was the temperature, the sounds, the smells?
- What clothes were you wearing?
- Who was with you?
- What did you say to those people, and what did they say to you?
- What took place? Recall as much detail as you can.
- How did this experience/transition/event shape your life?
- How has your life been different since then?
- What "things" helped you through this time?
- What "things" hindered you?

In response to these questions you might ask "how" questions, such as: How where you helped? How were you cared for? What things did people do to help you?

Summarize the conversation and the importance of the experience to the other person as he or she has named it. Ask if that is an accurate reading of the conversation for that person. Finally, decide in what way you will mark the significance of this conversation.

You might find it helpful to sit somewhere quietly after the conversation and write down what happened—not just a summary of the content of the conversation but what you did, what questions you asked, how you acted, and what effect that had on the conversation. Reflect on your intention in shaping questions and responses and their outcome in guiding the conversation. What questions emerge for you from your participation in this conversation? How will you see life differently as a result of this conversation? What questions will shape your future inquiry and learning? What do you see as your learning edges as a participant in pastoral conversation? How are your learning goals shaped as a result of participating in this conversation? This is important for engaging in deep conversation in the future.

12

Some General Conversations

THE FIRST MEETING

It is tough meeting someone for the first time and there is nearly always an uncertainty or anxiety about how you will be received. What if they think I just want to convert them? What if they don't like me? What if I don't like them? So many questions run through the mind. Such questions are normal. They are part of our anxiety. The important thing in creating a caring relationship or community is to know the people given to your care, and at the same time allow yourself to be known by those people. The "getting to know you" needs to be a two-way sharing.

In a first conversation ask questions for information.

- Tell me about . . .
- I was wondering . . .
- Where have you lived?
- Tell me about your life.
- What work do you do?
- Tell me about your family.
- What would you like to know about me . . . this community . . . this church . . . ?

Remember that "presence" is not about being right or dominant of others, it is about meeting them in a genuine and open and nonjudgmental way.

This initial conversation provides a starting point that will shape a future ministry of care, and future conversation. It is a foundation to build upon.

THE CELEBRATION CONVERSATIONS

In a meeting I heard a pastor say, "I make the crisis visits, and the parish nurse makes the long-term support visits." I wondered who made the celebration visits or whether they were not considered important. This is similar to the situation when ordained people are invited to the wake after a funeral. Often they will go because they believe they have a duty to care for people when they are hurting. But when invited to the party after a wedding they will decline to go, even see it as burden, because it is "only a celebration."

I think that we have fallen into the mistaken belief that people need support in times of crisis and they will survive well enough in times of celebration. Meeting with people to be in conversation about, to mark, and to celebrate the good times will show that we value all of life. The weddings of children are significant events in life, as the deaths of parents are significant events.

The questions to focus such conversations are simple: "Tell me about the wedding plans. What role will you have? What will make the celebration meaningful for you?" Or: "Tell me about the award you have been given. That is quite an accomplishment."

Look for appropriate ways to be with and to celebrate with people in the good times.

CONVERSATION AT KEY EVENTS

Birthdays, weddings, celebrations, achievements, anniversaries, when people move home, or when they migrate are key events that can be acknowledged. They become important times to make connection and be in conversation. You can ask people something simple, such as, "what does this event mean for you?" With more time you can focus your questions. If you are aware of these key events coming up then that is a good time to take the initiative to be in conversation. Focus your conversation around the importance of the particular event.

Special birthday

At a fiftieth birthday celebration I sat beside my friend, whose birthday it was, and said, "I am going to ask you to tell us what was happening in your life at five-year intervals." A group gathered, drank wine, and listened while he shared stories. He named his identity at an important milestone in his life and we heard some wonderful stories.

Moving

When people are leaving a home and moving somewhere new, you can ask all members of the family questions that will help them talk about how this place has been important and what moving will mean for them. Remember that each family member will have a different perception. Value each person by addressing questions specifically to each and listen while each one answers.

- What are the memories this home has for you?
- When did you come here?
- What have been the key events here?
- What spaces or objects are important symbols of your time here?
- What will it mean for you to leave this space?
- What will you do to celebrate your time here and to mark that you are moving on?

People move on in different ways. As people live longer, one of the movements is to assisted care or nursing home accommodation. When my dad moved into assisted care I became acutely aware that this meant the end of his cohabitation with his wife. It was a sad and lonely event. A conversation with both partners asking about their shared life and acknowledging this separation and movement would have been helpful.

CONVERSATION IN THE TOUGH TIMES

We all go through times that are tough and when we don't know how to ask for help. I remember such a time when I wasn't very open to acknowledging that I was having a tough time (though I was). A friend turned up on my front door step with a bottle of red wine and said, "You look as though you have been having a tough time and so I have come to share this wine with you."

If you keep your sensory antennae out you will know when people are going through tough times. The recognition doesn't have to be "heavy." A simple acknowledgment of your awareness is helpful, as can be a tentative question such as, "Would it be appropriate for me to visit or for us to meet for a coffee or lunch sometime? Give people room to say "Thanks for noticing, and no, I don't need a visit or conversation." That is not a rejection of you. It simply says they don't want to be in conversation at the moment. Similarly as you initiated the meeting you have to make sure that you remain available for the conversation. It leaves people hurting more if at the last minute you call to say you can't make it and then do not make an alternate time.

You can say, "You seem to be tired. It looks as if life is a bit hard for you at the moment. Tell me, how is life for you at the moment? At work? At home?" And then listen. Do not assume that because you think this person is having a tough time that he or she actually is.

CONVERSATIONS AT WORK

Christian community gathers for worship on Sundays and then disperses. In their daily work the people of God seek to live out their faith. By visiting them in their workplaces you are saying, "You are valuable outside the place of worship; you are valuable in your daily work." The conversation will be about what it means to be a person of faith in this work setting.

I learned what should have been obvious, that what the people were doing in their workplaces was crucial to the function of society. Their jobs involved looking after waterways, overseeing welfare, teaching in schools, being scientists, being lawyers, functioning as accountants and administrators, being in medical practice or nursing, doing social research, forming social policy, ensuring that foods were healthy, making clothes, and so many more roles.

In these settings, once you have taken the initiative to visit, all you really have to do is turn up. Your presence will be enough. The conversation will take care of itself because people are grateful for the pastoral contact and because at work they are very intentional about how they use their time. Sometimes it will be appropriate to offer pastoral prayer in these settings and sometimes not.

CONVERSATIONS ABOUT ETHICAL DECISION MAKING

Making ethical decisions is demanding and often lonely. People will seek and use a conversation with a pastoral person to think through what is right or wrong about decisions they have to make. Should I pay this tax? Should my son be responsible for the upkeep of the child he fathered, even though he did not know that the woman was pregnant? In my workplace do I have the right to name a worldview different from that of my colleagues? Should I go to my former husband's funeral when we separated forty years ago? How should I relate with my adult children who . . . ? I am hurting in my relationship and I am having an affair to meet my need for intimacy sexually and emotionally. I'm telling you because I want you to know, and I want to know what you think.

Often such questions come as a surprise, something you hadn't anticipated. Sometimes they challenge deeply your own chosen values. Such challenge threatens who you are and it is easy to find that you are arguing to defend your own view of what is right and wrong, when ideally you would like to be supporting the other person in his or her delicate decision making.

First of all listen with all your being. It will be difficult. Summarize the dilemma as you hear it stated. Check to see that you have understood accurately. Then if there is a churning in your chest about your own worldview on this matter, say to the other person, "Let me tell you what is happening inside me as I listen to you." If your own worldview is challenged, name how that challenges you and your chosen values, and then let it go. Many conversations like this will demand that you rethink your own worldview. Ethical decisions emerge from a conversation between the experience in the present, the received tradition which includes the Scriptures, and your faith tradition. Inevitably ethical dilemmas seem to shape a rethinking of how you understand the Scriptures and your tradition's faith stance.

Then help to clarify the decision. "So tell me again the dilemma for you." It is helpful for people to repeat themselves in this setting. The more times they speak about the dilemma, the more likely they are to clarify the dilemma. Telling you about this matter a second or third time will be helping them to become clearer. Summarize what you have heard: "As I hear it, your research has produced important information that the government wants to suppress. You are wondering if you should defy the government and release the information."

Then you can ask, "What shapes the values that are most important for you?" Our values are formed in multiple ways: our family of origin, our faith community, the schools we attended, the friendship networks we mix in, the dominant culture, the business we are in, and so on. Helping a person clarify values will help him or her make an appropriate decision. Your task is not to dictate what decision to make so much as to help the person come clearly to a decision that he or she will be able to live with.

Then ask, "What in your present context influences this dilemma?" Ethical decisions are often changed by context. My dad's highest value, I think, was being honest. The second highest would have been not to steal. Late in his life he told me how, when he was a prisoner of war, with no food, he resolved that he would never starve to death. In a different context he would steal in order to eat food and remain alive. The context influenced his ethical decision making.

Again, listen closely and summarize as best you can. "From what I can hear you saying your strongest values are about creating a just society, and about telling the truth. The dilemma is that you have important information the government doesn't want to release and you know that it will affect the lives of thousands of people."

When the issue seems not to resolve itself clearly, you could ask what personal story or story of faith comes to mind to inform this decision. Ask the person to tell you the story in his or her words. Don't worry about whether the story is accurate to the text or tradition. Understand that the way the person tells this story is right for the resolution of this dilemma—for example, one man said, "I always hear the story of Jesus crucifixion as being about his integrity to stand firm in the face of government opposition."

You could then focus the conversation on "How will that affect the decision you need to make?" or "What is the decision you are going to make?" When you have together talked around the subject (the other person mostly talking and you mostly listening), if you ask one of these questions it might surprise you how clear the response is. On the other hand, sometimes people need to sleep on their decision making and your conversation is merely one step among many.

It is possible that someone works through a decision with you, you both leave feeling how wonderfully helpful the conversation has been, and then a few days later the person makes the opposite choice. This is not a rejection of you, nor a denial of the value of the conversation that you had together—though it is easy to think that. It is simply that in that person's decision making there was a movement backwards and forwards as they worked through and owned the decision. That individual is most likely very grateful for your time, interest, wisdom, and help.

When the conversation is complete to the satisfaction of both, bring it to an appropriate conclusion. "How do you think you will act? How can I help and support you in your choice?"

13

CONVERSATION ABOUT FAITH AND LIFE

When you as a pastoral person want to focus a conversation on faith and life, any of the following questions might be helpful. There isn't a proper question or a proper sequence of questions. It is up to you to think how you might use one or more of these questions.

Remember that the questions that ask people to tell the stories of their own lived experiences give them power in the conversation. On the other hand questions about abstract and dogmatic concepts undermine confidence, because they are the currency of those who are particularly educated in these areas. Be aware that many people are intimidated by the particular knowledge and language of religious and theologically trained people. If you want conversations to flow, shape questions that begin with describing experience. Then it might be helpful to shape a reflective question, "How has that experience shaped your understanding of God?"

Here is a list of questions. Some are mine and some I have taken from James Fowler (1981).

Significant people in your faith journey

- Who first told you the stories of faith?
- Who prayed for you?
- What are the important relationships that you have had with people of faith and those not of faith? How would you describe those relationships?
- Who have been your mentors in faith and life? What are the stories you would tell of these relationships?

Important spiritual resources and practices

You could shape questions to explore the particular faith practices of the other person:

- In what ways and times has the Bible been particularly important for you?

- In what ways and times has prayer been important for you? In what ways has the nature of that prayer changed over time?

- What have been the spiritual disciplines that you have undertaken at various times in your life? In what ways have these disciplines nourished and sustained you? (Help people understand that walking along the beach in quiet thought, listening to music, writing in a journal, breathing quietly in the train on the way to work are spiritual practices. When you ask a question like this, be generous, be affirming, help people in their tentativeness to know that they are people of spiritual discipline and prayer.)

- What conversations have been particularly insightful and helpful for you? What is the story of those conversations?

- What have been the phases or chapters of your life? How have you changed your worldview and faith over time?

Cultural influences

Other questions might focus on broader cultural experiences that have shaped the person's understanding and helped him or her shape a worldview. The arts consciously and unconsciously shape our imagining and our faith.

- What books have you read (music have you listened to, movies have you seen, paintings have you looked at, dance and drama have you been party to) that have influenced significantly your understanding of life and the world?

- Are there particular writers or thinkers whose works have shaped you? Who are they and how have they influenced your life?

Encountering and being in conversation with others

We are shaped and formed by all that happens to us—the conversations that we have, the places we visit, the sermons we hear, and the places to which we travel. One of the most significant factors for changing our faith or worldview comes when we encounter difference. When people tell you about their encounters with difference, they are likely to tell you about how their thinking and worldview have been shaped. When I visited a third-world country and saw the ways in which people lived—old cars, bald tires, minimal road surface, small roadside stalls—I had to rethink the affluence in which I live. It shaped how I live as a person of faith. Helping people identify and name their encounters with difference can help them identify and talk about what is important in their faith.

- What are the sermons you have heard, the worship services that you have participated in, the study groups you have been part of, the camps and conferences you have shared in, that have been significant for you? In what ways have they shaped you?
- What travel, trips, walks, activities, and encounters have been important in forming who you are?
- In what ways have you encountered difference? How has your worldview changed as a result?

Moments of transcendence

All of us have had transcendent moments at sometime in our lives. That is, we have had experiences that somehow lifted us beyond ourselves to an awareness of something other. At first people might be reluctant, but then they slowly will tell you about times that were important to them. Moments of transcendence may connect with moments of despair.

- What have been the times of despair and doubt in your life? What has been helpful for living through those times?

- What have been the transcendent moments in your life?

These questions work together to name a person's faith. You could ask any of these questions, if the time is appropriate, and you would be helping the other to name his or her life, faith, and soul.

How do you introduce such questions? If there is nothing more specific to talk about you can float something like "I'd like to know a bit more about you . . ." or you could ask any of the previous questions: "Tell me about your journey of faith." Using some selected questions from the preceding list might help the other person to become more specific and to go deeper.

If you are going to ask these questions, give yourself time to hear and take seriously the answer. If you are interrupted before the answer is complete take the conversation back so the other person or people can finish talking. You need to be continually thinking what is the next or subsequent question that will enable the flow of their story, and then the questions that will enable the other person to keep talking and going deeper.

Be willing to summarize what you have heard others say, and affirm their integrity in thinking seriously about their faith. Value the willingness of people to think deeply and openly about life and faith. In so doing, you will be encouraging them to live their faith.

CONVERSATION AT THE TIME OF BIRTH

While in theological college I had spent time reading and thinking about the nature of death. As a result I was precociously willing to engage people about death. I had done no such study on the nature of birth, and so, I think, I inappropriately kept my distance. I went to visit people during pregnancy and in the hospital at the time of the birth. I didn't know what words to say, what conversation to have, or how to appropriately mark the event. It surprises me now when people remember that I visited them in hospital when their children were born.

I recall the time of the birth of my first child. I was pushed to silence. No words were adequate to express what the experience meant to me. Now, thirty-something years later I can see that my presence with new parents as a symbolic representative of God spoke in ways that I couldn't have at the time. By being there I was helping name and mark the significance of birth for those I visited.

When you learn that people are newly pregnant you can listen to their excitement and their anxiety. Do not assume that every newly expectant mother will be excited by her pregnancy; it may be that the pregnancy is unplanned and distressing for the mother-to-be (and father-to-be). You can shape questions that help to talk about joy, excitement, hope, anxiety, fear, anger, or bewilderment.

When the pregnancy is wanted, be present to hear the excitement and to celebrate:

- "You look and sound radiant. Tell me what it is like for you to be pregnant?" (Remember at these times, there are typically two people involved in the pregnancy, so you will want to shape a question to ask the partner about his experience too.)

- Help the couple to identify and name the hope that they have for this child.

- Be alert to anxieties and fears. When so much is hoped, people often also have great anxiety. "I can see this is a really exciting time for you; are there any anxieties as you move forward?"

- Check with the couple about the supports they have for the journey. Are there parents nearby? If not, what support systems do they have in place?

- Look for ways to celebrate the moment. Would a pastoral prayer be appropriate?

When the pregnancy is unwanted the conversation might take a radically different form. Be aware that it is not just out-of-wedlock pregnancies that are unwanted. A family might have their planned two or three children and then find that the mother is pregnant again and the pregnancy creates a crisis for the couple.

This can be a confusing time. Personal experience and personal values may make the conversation difficult. Let's say that the pastoral person has a thirty-five-year-old daughter who has been trying unsuccessfully to conceive a child; then having a conversation with a couple blessed with an unwanted pregnancy creates all sorts of internal havoc. This is why we have to be continually reflecting on how our own experience influences how we engage and respond in conversation.

First of all be present and listen. If necessary declare your internal dilemma without letting that take over the conversation. Then shape questions that honor the dilemma the couple faces. Listen with integrity. To the satisfaction of the couple, name the dilemma that you hear being spoken. Be aware that in relationship the couple may have different views about the dilemma that the pregnancy brings. When you have listened and you think it appropriate, draw the conversation to a close. Know that you cannot solve the dilemma by giving advice. If appropriate, offer a pastoral prayer that holds the dilemma before God.

Miscarriage

Sadly, life is vulnerable and fragile, and some pregnancies miscarry. This is the time for another most important pastoral conversation. Well-meaning people in the community often say things that hurt deeply: "It must have been God's will," "There must have been something wrong with the child; it is better this way," "You will be able to have another one." You will want to be present in ways that listen and bring the hurting couple to speech. Ask what the experience has been like. Encourage the people to tell the story of how the pregnancy miscarried. At different stages in the pregnancy the language used might be quite different. Be alert to the sense of loss this miscarriage brings to the couple. Help them to name the hope they had for this child. Ask them what name they have given or will give to this child. Ask what the name means for them.

When this conversation seems to have run its course it may be appropriate to ask, "How can we acknowledge the life of this child? Would it be appropriate to have a funeral rite of some sort to mark the death?" Be aware that appropriate ritual will grow from the conversation.

Joy

Birth itself is usually a time of great joy. At Christmas I become aware again of how the culture uses the anniversary of the birth of Jesus to celebrate birth and new life. Every birth seems to be acknowledged in the singing, the celebration, the feasting, the present giving, and the praise. I wonder how at the time of birth we can hear, celebrate, and name the joy that the event brings.

As always, the first task for the pastoral person is to be present and to attend with openness, to listen and to hear the experience of the parents. When you have listened and heard the parents, seek to find a way to acknowledge their joy before God. Being invited to clink champagne glasses with the parents of the newly born is as intimate a privilege as being invited to shed tears with the grieving.

Use the following to focus conversation on the birth:

- Tell me about your birth experience. (Let people tell you their story and resist the temptation to tell stories of other births. Give your attention to these people and their story.)
- How did you choose the baby's name?
- What is your hope (or prayer) for your new child?
- How will you celebrate this birth and mark it as a special moment?

In Western society there are no clearly recognizable rituals to mark birth. In the Pacific special parties are held on the first birthday.

Because in the past there was a high infant mortality rate people did not want to celebrate too soon, so they waited until the first birthday. That remains a significant cultural celebration. Helping new parents clarify how they will celebrate the birth (in their family) will be important. The next section on infant baptism reflects the need to separate a celebration of the birth from a ritual that marks entry into the Christian community.

CONVERSATIONS AT THE TIME OF INFANT BAPTISM

What questions might shape conversation when people are asking for infant baptism? Pastoral conversation is made more complex at this time because there is an overlay of a desire to have some ritual celebration of birth with the Christian symbol of baptism. Western society has few formal rituals to celebrate the special moment of birth. Parents approach the church for infant baptism, even though they may have no other connection with the Christian community.

Parents, perhaps, are most conscious of their unique connection with the creator God in the moment of birth and want to acknowledge that in the church. Parents also know that they want something special for their child and are unable to articulate clearly what that something is. I think they want God's blessing on this new life. All their unspoken wishes for this child, all their hopes for what they may be to this child, all their vision for what this child might become in the world are expressed in this, often uncertain, request for infant baptism. It is a deep prayer.

Different congregations have different ways of handling requests for infant baptism. I offer a suggestion as to how such a conversation might be shaped and hope that it stimulates you to think about how you do what you do.

People would often phone and ask if their children could be baptized. The request would be for the baptism to be on a specific day, usually because members of the extended family could be present. The first difficulty is that that day might not be convenient for the congregation and negotiation needs to be clear and open.

Baptism in my tradition is a community event and normally takes place within regular worship. The baptismal liturgy includes the active involvement of an elder who stands with the parents, representing the congregation.

As minister I would want to make a time to visit the family when both parents (normally) are home and when the congregational elder could participate.

Sometimes there is only one parent involved in the baptism. The first time a sole parent wanted a child baptized was a shock to me and I peculiarly wondered what the congregation would think. I hadn't yet been able to articulate that baptism is a symbol of God's acceptance of us whoever we are. Life changes us.

Where possible I would want this conversation about preparing for baptism to happen in the home of the family because the conversation is different when it happens in the space of the people making the request. Something good happens for people when visitors come into their space.

Such conversations most often happen in the evening and are difficult (for lay and ordained people) because they make the day stretch out. When the minister and elder share the conversation there is an opportunity to talk together about the nature and form of the conversation and to reflect together afterwards. This visiting by both is valuable and ideal, but not always possible.

When you visit you are entering someone else's space. How can you be present to the space and acknowledge the space to the people you are visiting? Young families often have new furniture, images, household things, all of which have their own story and allow you to make good connection with the people. If you are meeting the people for the first time it may be important to ask about their lives, to learn the story of who they are, where they grew up, how they met and chose to become parents. Find out too, about their work life. And when they ask, let them know about your life.

Be aware of the time available and the things you would want to achieve in the conversation before you leave. It is possible to name your agenda in making the visit. "We'd like to know about your experience of the birth and to talk a little bit more specifically about the baptism. We've got 'x' amount of time; is that okay with you?"

That lets the people know your agenda and that you will work to keep to that agenda and time. People often want to share a drink or something with people who come into their home. It is an important part of the conversation that you be open to receiving the hospitality that is offered to you. Receiving their gift empowers the people you are visiting.

There are lots of questions you can ask that will focus a conversation at this time:

- What was the birth experience like for you? (Make sure that you ask mother and father separately and hear different perceptions of the same event. This will facilitate an important conversation in the marriage.)
- Tell us about the birth.
- How did you choose the child's name?
- What significance does that name have for you?
- What do you hope or wish for your child?
- How do you feel about parenting?
- (You can say things like "Parenting the first time was a real culture shock for me. I didn't know just how demanding it would be" or something similar, so long as it is true.)
- How has the birth of your child changed your marriage relationship?

For me, asking this question became important because I had done some research on what happens to people in the leaving-home stage of the family life cycle. I understood that marriages often change radically at the birth of the first child. The couple becomes more focused on parenting and less on being a couple. That change is reinforced with the birth of subsequent children. If people do not work to maintain the intimacy in their marriage, by the time their children are themselves becoming adult and wanting to move out of the family home the parents are dependent on the intimacy with the children, and unable to let them go. The result is that these young people explode out of the family and the marriage is left in difficulty.

I saw the time of visiting to talk about baptism at the birth of the first (and subsequent) children as an important opportunity to coach parents that they needed to intentionally work on maintaining the intimacy of their marriage as a base from which to share mature parenting. Having a happy marriage is the best way to have happy children. New parents need permission to attend to and look after their relationship as a couple. Being perfect parents is a rising societal pressure.

The conversation needs to focus on what baptism is in the Christian community. Pastoral people have to be careful not to ask questions that the people they are visiting do not have the resources to answer. In this conversation if the pastoral person says, "Let me tell you how I understand baptism in the Christian community . . ." and then stays with a simple and accessible definition, there is a possibility of the parents responding to the knowledge that has been shared. I find it helpful to leave a small book about baptism with the family.

The conversation can then move to talking about the baptismal service specifically. Particular attention can be given to letting the people know what will happen in the service. If you give them a copy of the liturgy it is possible to go through the service together, using this as an opportunity to educate about the nature of baptism.

At some time in this conversation you will need to write down the specific information that goes on the baptismal register in the church and the baptismal certificate.

When the conversation concludes, seek to mark its pastoral nature. "Would it be appropriate for me to pray for your child and your home?" The pastoral people could choose simply to say, "God bless you and your home" as they leave, or they could say, "We look forward to sharing in the baptism." There isn't a right or wrong way to proceed. The important thing is that you act with integrity for you and for the people you are visiting.

Premarital Conversation

CONVERSATION WITH THE MARRYING COUPLE

One of the great privileges for people in ministry is to be invited to be a celebrant or conversation partner at the time of a couple's wedding. To conduct the wedding well will depend on your engaging a deep and open conversation with the couple being married. The conversation is sometimes exclusively the domain of the ordained person, and sometimes shared with or conducted solely by lay persons. The conversation is educational and can establish the tone of the marriage as people are given resources for sharing their lives.

The conversation begins when people make their initial contact. Give them as much information as you are able, remembering that information is power and you want to empower them to enter marriage well. Give information about legal requirements, church requirements, costs involved, and opportunities to prepare for marriage.

Your contribution to the subsequent conversation(s) will be enhanced by your knowledge of the human life cycle and the nature of marriage. Read about marriage from the social sciences and from theology. You can add to this experience by attending workshops or participating in courses that enable you to reflect with more discipline and more depth on the subject. That is the background preparation that makes the conversation possible.

I would offer a minimum of three meetings to couples preparing for marriage: the first to meet and fill out legal documents, the second to have a deeper conversation, the third to go over the finer details of the service. From the outset I would say to the couple, "We strongly encourage you to have some premarital education. A way to do that is to make a time with me in which we can talk about who you are in relation to your marriage. This is a really important thing for me to do. It will help me in conducting an appropriate wedding for you." Normally I would suggest an hour to an hour and a half for this conversation. I would add, "If you find it helpful and would like to take the conversation further, I will make time to do that with you, because I think it is very important."

In the first meeting with the couple I ask them to tell me their story in general terms. While I have collected some basic information that goes on government documents (name, age, place and date of birth, parents etc.), I ask them to tell me their story: "How did you meet? How did you decide to marry? Who asked whom?" I want them to be able to tell their story. In the first meeting these questions are tentative and help in us feeling comfortable with each other.

Shape your questions specifically and intentionally. "Mary, how did you first notice Bill? What did you notice? How did you respond? What did you feel? When was the first time you went out together? Bill, when was the first time you noticed Mary? When did you first go out together? How did you choose to marry Mary? And Mary, how did you choose to marry Bill?" In asking questions in this way, questions specifically to each partner about the one incident, I want to establish from the outset that it is possible for people in relationship to perceive the same event differently.

This early conversation could proceed in a number of directions. Have the couple been living together? If they have been living together I might ask, "How did you choose to live together?" If not living together, it is possible to ask other questions about value systems and choices: "Lots of people choose to live together before they marry these days. Tell me what shaped your decision to wait until you are married." If people are living together I might ask, if it seems appropriate, "Bill, when did you become married to Mary?" "Mary when did you become married to Bill?" It amazes me how specific people are in answering this question and how different it may be for each partner. If the couple can name that they are already married then it is possible to shape the conversation around the public celebration of a private commitment.

Listing birth dates prompts questions about age similarities or age differences. In listing the names of the parents of the bride and groom it is possible to shape questions about the life, death, and marriage of those significant others. This gathering of information always opens broader opportunities for conversation. At the conclusion of this conversation, for which I usually allow an hour, I give people a copy of the marriage service and invite them to think about how they want to structure a marriage service to celebrate their life together. I make a time to meet with them for a longer, more specific conversation.

It is important that people know in advance what will happen in a particular meeting. It allows them to prepare mentally and emotionally. "When we meet next time I would like to collect from both of you information that will help you talk about who you are in your family of origin. Then we will talk about what it means to join families in the act of marriage." I work to assure the couple that the conversation is not for me, but for them.

In the second meeting we spend significant time focusing on specific questions relating to their lived experience in their families of origin. They won't remember much, if anything, of the advice I give them. Most of the significant things they learn will happen out of the connections that they make themselves. I want them to leave continuing the conversation we have begun, together. So I say to people, "What happens in this room is not as important to me as whether you go away and continue this conversation about your marriage." For the marrying couple it is a lifelong conversation. My part in it is only an hour or two at most. I am here at its beginning, giving some permission, facilitating some questions. My other agenda is to plan and enact an appropriate marriage celebration growing from the conversation.

In the second conversation, I sit with a board and a large piece of paper on my knee to write down a lot of the things that I hear them saying about their families. I write on the paper the questions that I am asking them. At the end of the interview I give them this piece of paper to put on their wall or in their drawer. At some future time, I hope that they might look at the information or the questions and take up the conversation. Sometimes that will lead to pursuing the conversation with other family members. I reinforce that this conversation is for them, and not for me. My hope is that they will be talking about these things after they leave my office.

What underlies this conversation is my understanding that those entering into marriage need to know their own identity. When people know who they are they can live the transitions of their lives. The converse is also true; when people do not know who they are, it is very difficult to live the transitions of their lives. I work to help people know and name their identity by getting them to tell stories of their journey in family. Often they do not have all the information and are stimulated to be in conversation with parents and other family members to find out.

Marriage is the joining of families. Experience in a family, participation in its routines is what gives individuals security even when those routines are dysfunctional. Early conflicts in marriage often emerge because the individuals in the marriage have learned things differently in their respective families of origin. In one, birthdays are celebrated with a big fuss, and in the other they pass unnoticed. In the marriage a birthday comes and she takes no notice. He is devastated because in his family making a big fuss at birthdays says you are loved. She can't see the big deal. To talk about how these different families have celebrated birthdays can alert the couple to a possible tension. In time they will have to work out their own pattern for celebrating birthdays.

If you ask people how they understand marriage they will look at you in a dumbfounded way and will probably become inarticulate. If you ask them to talk about the family they grew up in they will be both confident and competent to speak. The most appropriate way to educate is to draw on what people already know, namely the experience of their own families. So the conversation emerges from what the people already know.

I begin the conversation by asking some specific questions of one member of the couple. Who I begin with is a matter of intuition. You have to begin somewhere and I begin often not realizing why I have chosen one over the other except that one looks more open, more willing, or because I just happen to be looking at that person at the moment.

During the conversation my antennae are out looking for patterns, looking for the teachable moment in relation to marriage and family. People choose a marriage partner from a remarkably small selection of possible partners. Usually people choose a partner who is complementary to them. This works, for example, in that a firstborn child may choose to marry a later-born child. Firstborn children are usually responsible, serious decision makers and late-born children can be less responsible, more playful, and willing to have others make decisions for them. When a firstborn and late-born child marry, there is a complementarity in the relationship. This can be a strength, and sometimes later on, as people change in their worldview and life experience, it can change. In my marriage I wanted somebody to mother me, and my wife wanted someone to mother. When children came we had to change that pattern quickly or our marriage would have crumbled.

The more you learn about the nature and function of marriage, the easier it will be to shape appropriate questions.

Factual information

- What is your birth date?
- What is your given name? How was your name chosen?
- Where did you come in the family?
- How many children are in your family?
- When were the others born? (This enables asking questions about how this family was planned. Ask questions about the irregular spacing of children.)

Perceptions

- Do you know how your parents planned their family?
- Do you know the story of why there are four years between the second and third children? Can you tell that story? (Where there is uncertainty encourage people to go and talk with their parents, and to ask questions for information.)
- How was it for you to grow up with siblings who were close together or far apart in age?

Facts about other generations

- What are your parents' names?
- When were they married?
- Do you know how they met?
- How did they choose to marry?
- What work do they or did they do?
- Are they still living? If not, when did they die? What was the circumstance of their death(s)? How have their deaths af-

fected you? Do you think that death affects the way you enter into this marriage?

- What are the names of your grandparents?
- When were they born?
- Are they still living? If not, when did they die?

Family relationships and crises

- What sort of relationship have you had with your grandparents? Which ones have you been particularly close to?
- What are the separations that have taken place in this family through breakdown of marriage or through employment or illness or war service or imprisonment?
- Who are the people that have died in the family? What was that time like for you? How do you remember that time?
- Have there been illnesses, hospitalizations? What was that time like for you? How do you remember that time?

Geographical movement

- What are the geographical movements of the family? Did the family migrate? What was their experience of migration?
- What language is the language of your bedroom?
- What language will be spoken in your home?

While many of these are factual questions, they allow you to offer the opportunity of a conversation that involves reflective thinking about experience in marriage and family. When people are helped to talk about the experience of the birth of a sibling, the death of a sibling, the separation of parents, the divorce of parents, the geographical movements, and so on, they are empowered to speak about their understanding of being in marriage and family.

Beliefs and family ethos

There are other series of questions that I find helpful to ask:

- What are the happy memories, the tragedies, the traumas, the crises, and the celebrations of this family?
- What is the religious belief and expression of this family (assuming that all families have some way of interpreting meaning)?

- What are the commonly told stories in this family?
- What is the political belief and expression of this family?

Rules and roles

- What are the written rules and the unwritten rules of this family?
- What are the roles of the members of this family?
- What is the role of a mother, a father, a husband, a wife, a lover, a son, and a daughter?

I want to distinguish very clearly the role of husband or wife from that of mother or father. Much of what people describe as the role of husband and wife will shape how they see the role of a husband and wife in the marriage that they form. When both stories have been collected, it is possible to have a conversation about how they would see the role of husband, wife, lover in their marriage.

Sexuality

- What sort of lovers do they think their parents were?
- How might they see the role of lover in their marriage?

Time and space

The questions to help people into conversation about various parts of their family are almost endless:

- How is space organized in your family?
- How do people organize time in your family?
- Could you describe the evening meal?

Such questions all enable a conversation about marriage.

Having entered into a significant conversation with one partner about his or her experience, I would then quite deliberately thank that person and move into conversation with the other partner.

As the conversation continues I look for patterns, in particular for significant differences between the two families. Then I facilitate a conversation about these things. Often people are sort of aware of these differences and uncertain as to how to talk about them. I want to create a possibility for them to continue a conversation around these matters after they have left my room. To this end, I give them the sheet of paper on which I have written the questions and particular information that I have collected from their family. One of the things that I find helpful to do is to write down particular phrases that I hear them say in response to the questions.

I make it clear to the couple that I would be prepared to continue this conversation further should they wish. I do leave the responsibility with them to ask. I want to be clear that when I ask people or invite people into a longer conversation, they do it not in order to please me, nor out of a sense of obligation, but because this conversation is important for them and they wish to continue it.

Sometimes the result of such conversations has been a concern that this is an inappropriate marriage. I think it my responsibility to say so when I think this. (Recall the conversation with the bride in the section on listening.) I say, "I have some concerns about you marrying." I do not send them away. I make it clear that I would be prepared to conduct the marriage. I want them to have a stable conversation in which to address difficult questions.

CONVERSATION WITH A MARRYING COUPLE AND THEIR PARENTS

In some situations I offer another dimension to this prewedding conversation by taking the conversation with this young couple into a conversation with their parents. Mostly I've done this where the families are members of my congregation. I do this because it enables a pastoral conversation to take place with other significant people at a moment that is important in their lives too. Marriage is more than a one generational event; it affects people in a number of generations of the family. It is particularly important for the parents of those children who are being married. It marks a significant transition in their lives. It is important for the couple entering into marriage to be able to relate to their parents as adults. Significant conversation with their parents around what it means to be married will help this. The conversation establishes a new way of relating that will be supportive for the couple in their marriage.

I typically offer to meet in the family home with the mother and father of either the bride or the groom. The marrying couple is present with one set of parents. I do not ask the bride's parents and the groom's parents together for this conversation as it generates an intimacy beyond the respective parents' relationship.

I would not have this conversation with parents who have divorced being present together, because their marriage relationship has ended and the conversation would require an inappropriate intimacy. This is an intimate conversation between parents and marrying children. Typically the conversation occurs in the evening and takes about two hours.

As I see it, my task is to facilitate a closer conversation between parents and marrying children, and to give people permission to break through the taboos in conversation that grow up through the parenting process. It is also to help the parents reflect on their marriage relationship at a time of significant transition. In talking with both parents and their marrying children I work to be clear about the agenda of this meeting and to give accurate information about how I would go about that. For the parents there is an opportunity to reflect on their marriage in the presence of their marrying children. For the marrying couple a supportive relationship is built in a new way with their parents.

Having outlined the purpose of the conversation to the parents and to the marrying couple, I begin with my first question in this conversation to one of the parents, "What's your recollection of when you met your partner?" There is often a lot of conversation with the eyes when I ask this question, of partners seeking to get their story right with their partner. I want to recognize that people's perception of their meeting, of their first date, of their decision to marry, and indeed of most things in their marriage and family will be different. So I encourage the one whom I have asked to tell the story the way he or she remembers it.

This conversation emerges as a "to and fro"; I will ask one the question and then the other the same question. I am not at all surprised that people have very different perceptions of their first meeting, especially after thirty years of marriage.

Then follows a series of questions around topics such as, "When did you first go out together? What's your memory of that? How did you choose to marry this person? What's your memory of becoming engaged? What's your memory of the wedding, the wedding day, the honeymoon? What's your memory of the early part of your marriage? These questions are really important because, while it's trite and obvious, the young couple is going through this stage of life at the moment. It is helpful when they recognize that this is something their parents have been through. Their parents have anguished over the same questions over which they are anguishing now.

Another series of questions might be about how they chose to have children: What were the circumstances of the birth? (If I have courage, and it seems appropriate, I might ask, "Can you tell us about the conception and birth of this family member who is to be married?") Talking openly about sexuality across the generations enables people to be adult together.

More questions might include ones such as: What have been the good times in this family? What have been the tough times? What resources did you as a couple draw on to survive the difficult times? And how did you celebrate the good times?

I encourage people to tell stories using lots of detail. If I ask a question about what might have been the difficult times, and the response seems short and brief: "When Mary was ill," "When Bill was laid off," "When Mary's Dad died," "When our children were ill," I ask, "Can you tell the story in more detail?" I would ask specific and open questions. "What happened to make that time difficult for you?" This requires some open-ended questioning, some encouragement to tell the story, and some attentive listening.

I want the marrying children to recognize the struggle in marriage of their parents/parents-in-law. I want them to recognize those resources their parents drew on and which ones were helpful for them. In this recognition the marrying children discover both their parents and conversation with their parents as sources for support in their marriage.

I also ask the parents how they feel about their child marrying, and what hopes and what anxieties they have for their children in marriage.

I recall the first time I ever did an interview like this. The interview was with the parents of the bride and the couple who was marrying. When asked if he had any anxiety about the marriage, the father of the bride said, "Yes, I have an anxiety," to the groom, "You're a Catholic. It's okay, though; you don't take that seriously." The groom, who had just been through a time of spiritual awakening quickly retorted, "Oh yes I do." It was a helpful conversation and the groom and the new father-in-law walked out of my house and down the front steps with their arms around each other.

In this conversation I am seeking to encourage the parents to talk openly about their marriage. I work to be in control of the conversation so that I might ask questions that aren't usually allowed to be asked (those about sexuality, conception, intimacy, conflict, meaning systems, and so on).

I ask the bride and groom what it's been like to listen to this conversation, what questions they have that they would like to put to their parents/parents-in-law. All the time I am seeking to develop a conversation between the generations. Sometimes as the last question I ask what names the marrying children should call the new parents-in-law.

When I think that the conversation has run its course, I offer an invitation to prayer. "Would it be appropriate for me to pray with you at this time?" If the people say yes, then I pray, giving thanks for marriage and the relationship of the parents, naming some of the specific things that I have heard, and praying a blessing on the marriage to be formed.

CONVERSATION IN SITUATIONS
OF CONFLICT

Conversations in times of conflict are sheer hard work. They are emotional and uncertain. Our breathing becomes shallow and our bodies shake.

I will always view with regret the first major conflict that I had with a congregational leader. In anger I threw the phone down, abruptly ending the conversation. I was under pressure and not coping. I was disturbed by the intensity of my anger and action. I went for a long walk past the home of the congregational leader. Though it was after 9 o'clock at night, I wanted to knock on the door and apologize, but I could not bring myself to do it. I was scared about how I would be received. The congregational leader left the church and, in spite of my later attempts to make contact and apologize, we have never spoken again. When conflict is handled badly relationships and communities are destroyed.

Subsequently I learned better ways to deal with conflict. The first step is to make time for a conversation. This takes courage and energy. You are probably thinking, "Why do I have to take the initiative? Why can't they contact me?" Being a leader demands that you take initiatives to resolve conflicts in the community. The sooner you act the better. Conflict isn't something you want to let fester. The sooner you deal with it the more likely it will be resolved in a healthy way.

If the conflict is directly with you then you need to say clearly, "There seems to be some conflict or a tension between us, and I'd like an opportunity to talk about that. I value your role in the community and don't want this conflict to continue. When would be a good time for us to get together?" When you do get together a good starting point would be to reiterate the comments you said when you set up the conversation: "There seems to be some tension between us . . ."

In situations of conflict be aware that there are high levels of anxiety and emotion for both participants. Consequently, where your meeting takes place and what happens in it are extremely important. Choose a place where you can be both comfortable and safe, and where you will not be interrupted. I found that for me the best thing was to arrange to meet in the home of the other, where that person would be secure. Asking him or her to come to my home would make me more powerful and increase his or her anxiety.

In the story of John and Daniel (chapter 7), I talked about what to do when people are angry and emotional. It offers some important suggestions about what to do in times of conflict.

In your speech be gentle in sound and slow down, not a lot, just a little. If it is too emotional and you or the other person seems out of control say so. "I am really bubbly inside and very emotional at the moment. It would help me if I could be silent and still for a minute or so to collect myself." Take the time and breathe gently and slowly. Let go of the arguments in your head and focus on relaxing your body.

Listen openly to the other person. This is not easy. Such a stance is uncertain and emotional. If you can listen so that the other person knows that his or her point of view has been heard, then you can move on. These conversations are never helped by argument. It is not about particular points of view being right or wrong. It is about listening and hearing the other and acknowledging that person's point of view. Hearing the story of how the conflict emerged for the other will be important. "I'd like to hear why this issue is important for you. Tell me how you see or understand it." Go slowly and listen intently.

As you listen be wary of using clichés. Saying "I hear you" will not resolve conflict. Only when you can satisfactorily name the other's point of view to his or her satisfaction will that person be heard. Acknowledge too, the other's pain. "I am aware of how much you are hurting over this issue." Only say things that are true for you. Have integrity, be honest, and be truthful in your conversation.

Summarize as clearly as possible. Allow people more time to clarify. Understand that people become much clearer in thought when they verbalize things. When they tell the story of the conflict, some of the energy is dissipated in the telling of the story. People will relax when their point of view has been heard and acknowledged.

Be listening for other issues too. People might be expressing anger about one issue when the anger is really about something else. In the story about my hanging up the phone on a congregational leader very little of my anger had to do directly with him. I was exploding inside over other issues in my life. I wanted someone somewhere to hear me. I cried out in an inappropriate way.

When you think that the other person is satisfied about being heard and acknowledged, then you might state your own view. Tell the story of how and why you came to your point of view. You are not mustering an argument; you are describing your perception of an experience. Name if you can, gently and softly, what is common and what is different in the two views. As you listen and talk, be alert for what things you hold in common. What you hold in common might be that you both want the good of this community. Be thinking about how you can facilitate your movement towards reconciliation, which will be shown in your ability to work together in and for the community.

When you think that you are finding common ground on which you can move ahead, you can bring the conversation to a conclusion. Remember that you do not have to come to a common view to resolve conflict. What you are looking for is an ability to hear and acknowledge and live with different points of view.

How could you use the resources and practices of faith to help complete and resolve this conflict? Is there a biblical story that could name reconciliation for you both? Would it be appropriate to pray? If in the conflict either or both parties have been offended or hurt by the other, what will be required for the people to experience forgiveness? How might that forgiveness be verbalized?

Until now, I have been talking about when you as an individual are in conflict with another individual. But conflicts also arise among people in community, and sometimes you are asked to help other people resolve conflict.

Conflict and change

In community conflicts often arise when change is being suggested. I have been amazed at the amount of energy people have when physical changes to a worship space are suggested. "If you move that communion rail it will be over my dead body!" "If you move that pulpit

I will leave the church." There are threats in the responses. The threats function like hooks and it is easy for others to get caught in them. Soon emotions escalate and tempers rise.

Respond slowly and gently. Breathe in long and slow breaths. "Tom, I can hear that this is a really important issue for you. Can you help me to know why or how it is so important for you?" Perhaps you can name how scared you become (if it is true) when people spring change on you, and how, after your initial resistance, you come to appreciate the importance of the change. Follow the pattern of the conversation outlined above.

Marital conflict

There will also be times when you are asked to be a conversation partner for people who are in conflict. A married couple comes to you and asks you to help them in their conflict. This can arouse all sorts of anxieties: "I am not qualified to do this," "I am too close to them," "I have enough trouble handling conflict in my own marriage," and so on. In approaching you, they are asking you to help because they trust you. Be complimented by that trust. Offer to sit with them to help them work out how they might proceed together. Find a place that is safe and where you are not likely to be interrupted. Ask each person in turn to tell you about the conflict. After each one speaks ask the other to say back what they have heard as accurately as they can, before they say their bit. Check with the first speaker to see if they have been heard accurately. Move on in this way until both partners feel that they have been adequately heard.

In bringing the conversation to a conclusion you can focus the couple on how they might get some more professional help. Here it is possible to voice the questions of your earlier anxiety: "I am not qualified to work with you on this, and I will help you find a good counselor." "You are too close to me for me to fulfill this role in any ongoing way. I am glad you trusted me. I hope that this conversation has been helpful. I will support you and come and see how you are getting on." Don't discount that your facilitative listening might have helped resolve the conflict and the couple no longer needs professional help.

Conversations are always ongoing. If someone tells you about the conflict in their relationship or asks you to be involved in the way mentioned in the previous paragraph, then be open to continuing the conversation. When you see them and there is an appropriate opportunity ask, "How are things at home?" I have found that a good way to ask about tensions in a marriage is to say, "How married are you today?" "Do you want to talk about that a bit?" It is important that you continue conversations like this for some time. To become silent with people who have shared their lives with you is often received as a judgment and invites conflict. Find opportunities to ask discretely how the people are journeying.

PREVENTING CONFLICT IN COMMUNITY

Churches are voluntary organizations with lots of meetings. Often meetings are places where emotions run high and conflicts surface.

At parish council a colleague minister and a lay leader were visibly upset. It wasn't possible to address their distress in the meeting. I chose to go and be with each sometime after the meeting, not because I had to go, but because this is how to maintain or create a quality of community and to avoid festering conflict. In each case the task was to name that I observed them to be upset and to ask if they would like to talk about that. The important thing was that I had to take the initiative to make an opportunity to have a conversation with each of them.

Similarly, in another church council meeting the superintendent of the Sunday school resigned. He seemed immediately to come under attack from three or four of the elders. It seemed to me reasonable for him to say, "I have finished what I can do in this role or task." In face of the attack the Sunday school superintendent stood his ground, which made for a tense and uncomfortable meeting. After the meeting each of these people needed to be contacted by me as minister. They needed help in talking through and moving beyond this experience. Most of all they needed someone to hear that they were not only finding burdensome their existing church responsibilities, but were now also angry about the resignation because they thought it would cause even more responsibilities to fall on them. The former Sunday school superintendent had to be affirmed in his decision to resign, and assured that there would continue to be a place for him in the community. As minister I had to be aware that there would be a lot more happening in the lives of each of these people than what appeared on the surface in a church meeting.

If you are alert and open you can do preventive things. When you know there are contentious meetings coming up, make conversational contact with the various persons beforehand. Phone them, say hello. When people feel heard and acknowledged they are less likely to enter into conflict. A proactive reaching out by pastorally sensitive people can lessen the possibility of conflict.

Structure some time into the meeting during which people can name the issues in their own lives. Many people come to meetings with a desire to be heard. If they aren't heard, they can commandeer the agenda of the meeting. Very quickly there is conflict in the meeting and no one is sure how to proceed. The one who wants to be heard moves a "strange" motion that consumes the community's energy for a significant period of time. When people have been enabled to talk about their own lives and have a sense of being heard and taken seriously they are much less likely to speak just for the sake of speaking.

People come to meetings with precious experiences that are not easily discernable. "Today I learned that my brother and his wife separated." "Today my work colleague's partner was diagnosed with cancer." People need to be able to name and be heard in the emotions these experiences raise for them. When they are heard and acknowledged, they function more easily in community. When they are not heard they often say and do things in meetings in order to be heard.

So make a time in the meeting for people to name the important things happening in their lives. You will defuse the possibility of conflicts arising. You can suggest that people talk with those near them naming the important things happening for them, and then ask if there is anything they would like to share with the whole community.

Contact people

When you have seen people hurting or angry at a meeting, be in contact with them afterwards. This is a task for lay and ordained people. The contact shouldn't be political ("I'm on your side, count on me"), but rather along the lines of: "I noticed that you were upset (angry, confused, hurting, etc.) at the meeting last night and I want to check how you are feeling about that now." The task is to notice, and to acknowledge, and to listen and hear people who are hurting.

Share information

Another thing that helps prevent conflict in communities is giving people access to all the information all the time. When people know things they are less likely to get into conflict. When some people hold particular information that is not available to all, then conflicts occur. Work to share information as widely as possible.

Allen

Conflicts also arise because we wrongly assume the other thinks certain things. Someone tells us that a certain person is upset about something. Without checking the source we believe the rumor, and in our minds begin to fight. I remember visiting Allen after a painful meeting. People had fed me the line, and I had believed them, that Allen would oppose a certain action. Someone had taken him to task before the meeting and he was deeply hurt. Within the meeting he acted with integrity to find the best way forward for the community. Knowing how hurt he had been in the meeting, I went to visit him. When I listened I realized how unhelpful it had been for me to believe what people had told me without my talking with Allen directly. When we met we spoke clearly, openly, and with tears, in ways that clarified our understanding of each other's point of view. In the conversation I heard about some of the welfare work Allen did and accepted an invitation to visit and see him in action. Our conversation led to his healing and the resolution of a conflict in the community's life.

To summarize: in situations of conflict take the initiative to make contact with the conflicting parties, be present to them, and listen openly. Don't try to change viewpoints. Affirm, acknowledge, and build up conflicting people. Look for ways to name the conflict and find ways to move ahead.

CONVERSATION AFTER A MARRIAGE SEPARATION

Being friends with and supporting people through marriage separation is another "tough" conversation. Marriage is a mystery to me, and from outside I can never see the pain that people are experiencing within marriage. When lived well, marriage enhances both partners' ability to live life abundantly and when lived badly the pain is such that it can lead to sickness and death. It is hard work for people to leave a marriage and only done after it becomes unbearable for at least one of the partners.

I begin such conversations with the belief that if both people have the will and energy they can get help and work through the present difficulties. If one of the partners does not have the will there is no way that the marriage can be made work. I have a basic belief that when one person takes a different position in a marriage or family then the other people have to take different positions. If it seemed appropriate I would use the conversation to coach a person to take a different position in their marriage in the hope that that might free up the pain in the relationship. Alongside this I believe that it is easier for a motivated and strong person to make changes than a hurting and defensive person. I work with the one who is with me, and whom I perceive to be strong because in some way that one is asking for help. "You seem to want your wife to organize your romantic life. What if you did it differently and you organized a babysitter and a night out? You are the one who really wants it, you are a good manager at work, why not bring that skill into the home?"

If people are resolved to separate, there is nothing that you can do to stop it. So the task is to listen and support the people in what will have been an anguished choosing for them. You need to acknowledge the hurt and pain of the relationship, the difficulty of choosing this action, and the efforts they have made to resolve the relationship. Be aware of and acknowledge the guilt that people feel when they have made lifelong commitments, in a public ceremony, in the presence of family and friends, and now cannot continue to live those commitments. Listen, summarize, affirm, and, where appropriate, mediate forgiveness.

The nonnegotiable separation

Alternatively you may be supporting a person who has valued the long-term commitment of marriage and whose marriage partner wants a separation and will not negotiate in any way. Give people permission to be in this situation. If a person has come to this moment with a strong personal value that he or she is committed to the marriage partner for life and the desire of their partner is for a nonnegotiable divorce, then there is a great moral dilemma that needs addressing. I think marriage was created for joy, not pain. In the conversation I will look for an opportunity to say to the person, "I know that you have some really well-grounded and strong values in relation to marriage. I can see how you have lived those values in the marriage (and I will name examples of how I think that has been so). It is alright for you to let the marriage go. The marriage is causing more pain than joy. You have lived your commitment to the best of your ability. The failure is not so much individual as relational. You are forgiven." I then try to look for words that would allow this person to move beyond guilt to responsible freedom. I want to find ways that enable the person to move beyond a sense of failure, beyond the guilt of not being able to live his or her own chosen values, to where that person can experience forgiveness and new life. The conversation should move beyond the mere saying of "You are forgiven" to facilitating an experience of forgiveness.

Of course it is easier for me to say this than it is for people in the marriage to let go. Letting go of a marriage to which people are very deeply committed is very hard emotional work. Even in hurting marriages people have shared special and intimate times. The memory of the good times is part of the identity of each partner, and in some way they will want to hold on to the possibility expressed in those memories. It is not easy to let that go.

These conversations need lots of time and they can stretch out over months. All you can do is be present, listen, support, and encourage with patience. How can you help this person accept the reality of the present situation and move on in life in ways that are safe, healing, and that offer the possibility of new life? You will have to have thought through your own understanding of marriage and separation. You will not be able to fix things. You can slowly listen to and hear about the confusion and pain of the present and help to clarify ways that this person can move on without hurting himself or herself or the people around him or her.

Engage in the conversation knowing that when the people entered the marriage and made the promises they did so with integrity and with every intention to fulfill the promises. Leaving the marriage will have a sense of failure for both partners and they will need help in conversation to acknowledge the failure. Listen for how people are hurting and help them to name that.

In conversations with people after a separation or divorce it may be appropriate to have that conversation flow towards the structuring of a public ritual to mark the end of the relationship. Since the relationship has irretrievably broken down it is probably not appropriate to try to involve both partners (but it may be). This ritual could be organized in conversation with an ordained person.

CONFESSION AND FORGIVENESS

There will be times when people want to tell you things about their lives that are difficult for them to say, and they come across as unburdening or letting go. They need to share with someone a difficult, embarrassing, uncomfortable episode in their living. They don't usually begin the conversation, "I need to confess something . . ." Confession often comes at times when trust has been built and the other person knows that he or she will be heard and taken seriously. What more often happens is something like this: Standing on the church steps after a Sunday service when most of the people have gone home, an inwardly hurting and confused woman began a conversation with me. She had seen a television program exposing a certain evil in society. She mentions in a vague kind of way that in her youth she had done something similar. It wasn't even clear to me what she was talking about. I listened and then suggested I visit her at home and we have a longer conversation. She accepted my offer, and so we talked.

I had to be proactive in raising the issue. "On the church steps you mentioned . . . , and I thought there was some more that you wanted to say about that." She talked, telling the story of the events that troubled her, and I listened, careful not to diminish the seriousness of the action. I listened openly, without judgment. I listened knowing that in the fragile thing we call life, in the same circumstance I may have done exactly the same thing. I listened as this person talked of her guilt. At the conclusion of the conversation I shaped a pastoral prayer around the prayers of confession and the declaration of pardon used in Sunday worship.

All of us have need at times to make confession in ways that are more particular than Sunday worship allows. At those times, be present to the other, be alert, and listen without judgment. Sometimes the confessing person will then need to be asked, "How can you be responsible for your action? How can you act to put this right?"

One Friday afternoon I sat in my home in conversation with a married couple. One of the partners had had a long-term affair. It was now in the open. The other partner was willing to forgive and get on with the marriage. The one who had had the affair was unable to forgive himself and the relationship had become stagnant. At the time I thought to myself, "This person needs a service in the church where they can make confession of their sin and hear a priestly person declare: 'You are forgiven.'" Though I thought those things I seemed unable to act on them. Having thought it through further, next time I wouldn't hesitate. I would say, "Why don't we have a small service where you can make confession and hear a declaration of pardon?"

Confessional conversation emerges in the informal and unguarded moment when the other person feels safe enough to risk revealing the deeply troubling thing. Be alert. Be open. Recognize when people are trying to say something in a different way. Value what they share. Don't judge them. You do not have to approve the action but you can listen. What feelings can you discern and name? Is there guilt and shame? What reparation will be appropriate? What will it mean for this person to be forgiven? How will you, as a symbolic representative of God, mediate forgiveness?

CONVERSATION IN HOSPITALS
AND WITH THE DYING

HOSPITAL CONVERSATION

Hospitals are places where sharp existential questions are shaped. Many of the conversations reported in this book have had their genesis in a hospital. It is in hospitals that most people are born, suffer, and die, so it is no surprise that deep existential questions are often shaped in hospitals.

While conversations might at times be deep, at other times they are difficult, especially for the inexperienced. How long should you stay when someone is ill and tired? What is it like for a patient who has a group of visitors, none of whom know each other? How do you find privacy for personal and intimate conversation in such a public space?

Early on I found conversations in a public ward of a hospital difficult. There were often four or five other patients in the room. All these ears and eyes I thought were focused on me and what I was doing. People in pajamas in bed were somehow threatening to me. The noise and interruptions of the medical staff made me feel awkward. If I went at visiting time often there were other people present and conversation was strained. What was my purpose in coming? Should I pray in these settings and with all these people watching and interrupting?

It can be helpful to phone the hospital and the patient and ask when would be an appropriate time to visit. Be discerning about when you visit and how long you stay when you go to see people in hospital. Sometimes you will have long and deep conversations and other times people will be pleased that you have come and glad that you only stayed a minute or two. When visiting, clergy might make contact with the nursing staff and indicate a willingness to be called should the particular person you are visiting request it.

When there are a lot of people around a hospital bed it is very demanding for the patient. This is especially so when the people do not know each other. The patient has to facilitate a conversation between strangers. Staying in these circumstances simply adds to the problem, so greet and leave. You might suggest coming back at another time; if so, be sure you actually do return.

People in hospital are ill and not likely to be functioning optimally. Being present to them is important. "Is it alright for me to sit with you for a time? Don't try and make conversation with me." On leaving it can be appropriate to ask, "Can I bless you?" or "Could I pray with you?" A blessing might involve simple touch, hand-holding or making the sign of the cross on the forehead and saying "God bless you." In some circumstances I use the Aaronic blessing (mentioned earlier, from Numbers 6:24–26.) My preference is for prayers to be short and to the point.

Because people are not well they will not necessarily want to engage in long conversations. Yet every situation is unique and you have to listen carefully and be discerning as to what is appropriate. Hospitals and medical procedures raise questions about the purpose of life and death, the nature of the body, the nature of healing, how people live with pain, why God allows suffering, and so on. If you are alert you will find ways to enter conversations that are life-shaping around these issues. Such conversations will require more time and this is for you to discern.

You can ask, "How are you feeling about this procedure?" Listen for, and respond to, the anxiety of people in these situations. If you visit people after an operation you can give thanks for medical skill and help people talk about how their lives will be different (positively and negatively) as a result of this procedure.

CONVERSATIONS WITH PEOPLE WHO ARE DYING

In hospital you are also likely to have conversations with people about their dying.

There are, I think, at least two stages in talking with people about dying. The first is a look back at life in which people seek to integrate

140

their life experience. The second is to look forward to, to anticipate, to enter the moment that is death.

When people use conversation for looking back and telling the story of their journey through life, the listener is often taken by surprise. It is easy to pass it off as "they are old, and they spend a lot of time remembering the past." An alert pastoral person will be attuned to the importance of the moment. They will work to help the person tell the story of their life's journey in ways that integrate, hold together, and make sense of the journey. It is as though to complete the journey properly people need to be able to hold up their life and look at it.

To have this conversation, ask questions that help people tell their life stories, and then listen: "Tell me about your childhood." "Tell me where you met your marriage partner." "Tell me about your wedding day," and so on. Sometimes the stories people need to tell most are the ones that don't make sense: experiences of war, disaster, separation, shame, abuse, and the experiences that until this time have been held as secrets. I remember an elderly person telling me about being gang raped in her youth, "but we didn't talk about those things then, so I didn't tell anybody." The revelation made sense of what had been difficult to understand in her life. She died a short while later.

When people have been able to integrate their life story, they will be able to live into their dying in fuller and richer ways, ways that reflect what Jesus meant when he talked about living life abundantly.

If someone is soon to be married it seems reasonable and even to be encouraged to ask about the wedding. If someone is facing their own death, it seems taboo to talk about it. Why would it not be appropriate to talk with them about that?

I find it difficult to know how to shape appropriate questions. I want to be sensitive, I do not want to be invasive, and at the same time I want people to know that I am willing to engage the subject of their dying if that seems appropriate to them. The boldest way may be the simplest. Why not just say: "If you want to talk about your dying I will be willing to talk with you." Then be patient. It may not be until a later conversation that the person takes you up on your offer.

Myrtle

Myrtle was in her late seventies and lived in an efficiency apartment in the high-rise apartments adjacent to the church. She was actively involved in the community and we had a good rapport. There was always a bit of a joke between us. She thought I was always "rattling her marbles," a colloquial metaphor for making her think about her death. I recognized that this was her way of saying to me that she was scared about death, so I made a time to visit her in her home. She told me the story of the death of her husband. He had been a patient in a local hospital. Because he usually listened to the races on a Saturday afternoon she chose not to visit until the evening, when she was informed that he had died. It was very distressing to her that he had died alone when she could have been with him. Older people living alone are often scared that they might die alone in their rooms and not be found for days. Some time later Myrtle came to me at the church. It was lunchtime. She said to me, "It is alright, now. I understand. I saw a television program last night." "Understand what?" I asked. She said, "About death."

That afternoon Myrtle went back to the high-rise with a group of friends. They sat together in the common space downstairs. She asked them to wait for her while she went upstairs to her room. After ten minutes, when she hadn't returned one of the friends went up to find her. The door was open. Myrtle was lying on the bed. She had had a heart attack and died. She had died with her friends nearby. I learned so much about life from this ongoing conversation. It was a gift that shaped me, giving me wisdom about how people live and talk about their dying, then die appropriately after having been given a chance to talk about it.

As people often talk about death in metaphors (like Bruce in the opening story), be wary of judging them when you are uncertain as to why they are talking this way. The pastoral person must begin with the assumption that people's reality is real for them, and the things that they are saying mean something for them.

The orchid

My dad was dying. My mum said, "It is lonely. He can't give me anything any more, and I have nothing left to give him." He had wanted money in the previous week to buy her an orchid. I reminded her of the orchid. She told me how she had given the money to my sister-in-law who bought a nice orchid for her. I held up the symbol of the orchid as perhaps the ultimate thing that he could give her. Perhaps it would be important to "touch the gift of the orchid." When Mum then told me how the first gift he had ever given her was an orchid, I couldn't control my tears. The appropriateness of the gift jumped out; the first and the last gift of the relationship, the completeness of life. Is this what Jesus meant when he talked of "abundant life?"

What questions might help a pastor reach into the deeper spaces surrounding death? The first questions might be helpful with someone who is dying. Remember that the questions emerge from a developed and developing relationship. In order to talk with people about their dying you usually have to have established a ground of trust that will be the foundation for a most intimate conversation.

- Do you have a vision or understanding of what death is?
- How do you see your own death?
- What are the images you have of death? (Some people tell about those who have died being in a special place, calling them to be with them. Some talk about fences or walls and they are seeking a way through and how they cannot find it yet, or the gate is too small to get through. Others talk of seeing all the family and friends who have previously died being in a green field, and being called by them. At the same time they have an awareness of doctor and partner holding them back saying it is not time yet.)

Take the time to write reflectively about your conversations. Write down the conversation. Look at the patterns, look at the imagery, think how the conversation impacts you and your experience. Each time you have a conversation with someone who is dying it adds to your wisdom about life. Often we only see the patterns in retrospect, that is, after the person has died.

19

CONVERSATION AT THE TIME OF DEATH

The phone rings, and the voice on the phone tells you that someone has died. It may be a person you know well, someone with whom you have an existing relationship on which you can build. It is equally possible that the one who has died is someone you have never met, and in your role as pastoral person you are asked to visit because of the death, and perhaps also to conduct the funeral. This will mean visiting with a family whom you may never have met and helping them to have an intimate conversation with each other about the death and funeral of someone they have loved dearly. It is a demanding thing to do. You have to build a pastoral relationship from scratch in a very short space of time.

The conversation with family members immediately following the death is likely to focus on planning and enacting a funeral. Your task is to be present, to listen, to guide as appropriate.

The first thing is to call the family member responsible and ask when would be an appropriate time to visit:

"I have just learned about Bill. I'm sorry. Could I come and visit? When would be an appropriate time?"

"My name is _____ , I am a minister of _____ church. The funeral director has just rung me to tell me about the death of your wife (or other family member. I'd like to come and visit to talk with you about the funeral. When would be an appropriate time?"

Think in terms of at least two visits before the funeral, though this is not always possible. It is important to have as many of the family present as possible for those visits. You, as the pastoral person, are the facilitator of a conversation in a family. Seek to make a time to visit when other family members are present. "Would it be possible for me to meet with you when as many of the family as possible are present? I'd be willing to facilitate a conversation where you talk together about how you remember _____. We will use those stories to shape what is said in the funeral service."

When you visit at the time of death it is easy to get caught into being the practical helper, for example, taking over the kitchen and making drinks. In the shock that follows death and other trauma, people need to do "ordinary things." They might get distracted while boiling the kettle, the cups and saucers might rattle in their hands, but it is helpful for people to be doing things. Letting someone make a cup of tea enables them to be competent in a small thing when it seems their world is collapsing around them. Part of what makes conversation pastoral is your ability to "be." In the midst of the chaos that follows death, trust yourself to sit in your own discomfort at being inactive. Be present, and listen. Your ability to "be" is what is important.

As a pastoral person, see your task as facilitating this family to engage in a conversation that will enable them to plan the most appropriate funeral, and to acknowledge and celebrate the life of this family member in the most appropriate way.

Because time is short, preparation for this conversation is sometimes limited to what happens in your car as you drive to the home and what you think as you walk up the path to the door. What am I going to say? Am I going to sound trite? What can anyone say that is helpful in the face of (this) death? What is my purpose here? What can I do? How should I greet these people? A handshake? A hug? What is appropriate intimacy? What is appropriate distance? How will I read the signs about what is appropriate for me to do? Can I acknowledge that I am anxious because I do not know what to do or what will happen? All of these questions find their way into a prayer that commits the imminent conversation to God.

The role you have of being invited into the intimacy of this family at the time of death is very privileged. Be aware of the privilege. This is difficult to sort out. I need to name for me that in parish ministry there was a strange sense that I knew most "who I was as a minister" when I was conducting a funeral. These people needed me and invited me into this most intimate place in their lives. If I do not name this strange inner need of mine, then it is easy for this need to get in the way of my working for and with the other. Not to be aware of how this meets my inner need, or not to name this (to myself) is to live a delusion. I am then at risk of using the invitation to share in this funeral for satisfying my own needs. When I do that, I will be less available to the other, and using the conversation solely to meet my need to feel important.

The first task in the conversation is to hear the story of these people. Let them tell you the entire story. You only have to ask what happened and, because of their need to story the event, the family will tell you. The circumstances of the death will shape this conversation. Before you can conduct the funeral you need to hear their story and, more important, the family needs to have told you the story.

When you meet with the gathered family it will be important for the family to hear each others' stories and experience. Remember that people always experience the same event differently. There isn't a right or wrong experience. Each will have an experience that is unique and each will need that story affirmed as important. Because emotions are raw at the time of death, it is easy for family members to be in conflict over what happened. They don't outwardly say someone is wrong, but one person will tell their story louder and talk over the top of another member, who tells the story differently. As a facilitator of a family conversation you can help by telling the family that it is normal for people to see the same event differently, and each telling is appropriate. When the family members can tell each other their unique stories and be heard and affirmed then the family grows in intimacy and strength to support each other through this difficult time.

It is also important to keep in mind that many people have a unique relationship with the one who has died, and all the relationships are different and need to be acknowledged: husband, wife, daughter, son, brother, sister, grandparent, grandchild, brother-in-law, sister-in-law, partner, lover, friend, and so on. Each will want his important relationship, her story, heard and acknowledged. For example, ask the grandchildren, "What was Pa like as a grandfather? What do you remember doing with him?"

Have in mind questions like these: How did she die? How did you learn of the death? Where were you when she died? Where were you when you learned of her death? When did you last see her? What was that like for you? What did you talk about? Do you think that you have said good-bye? What remains to be said? How can we appropriately acknowledge and celebrate this life? What will sustain you through this difficult time?

With some of these questions you have to be very aware of the multiple levels of conversation. In the section "Conversations with People Who Are Dying," in the previous chapter, I mentioned how when the experience of painful things is so close, people often talk in metaphors without realizing that that is what they are doing. They create images in their speech that enable them to integrate their experience. If you are appropriately alert to these other levels of meaning you can help people to see the appropriateness of their own stories and you will be able to plan with them an appropriate funeral service.

When you read/think that the time is appropriate, you will introduce the topic of the funeral. The conversation could go something like this. "Let's talk about the funeral. The funeral belongs to you as the family. My task, as minister, is to help you acknowledge your (family member's) life in the most appropriate way for you. I come as a Christian minister, so I will want to set that (acknowledgment of the life) in the context of the consolation of the Christian funeral service. What I want you to know is that you have a lot of power in this service to do what is important for you. In the old days when a family member died the men of the family went out and physically dug the grave together. We seem to have given over that right today. Yet it was really important. By planning for how the funeral will most appropriately meet your needs I hope that you can begin the process of saying good-bye to this family member. Saying good-bye is a slow process that begins with the funeral. If you do this well now, in time you will move on appropriately.

"You might like to think about things that will make this service important for you. You could choose some symbols that represent your (family member's) life. There may be some special things that represent who (he or she) was that you'd like to place on the coffin or a table in the front of the church. Your children (or all the members of the family) may be able to bring these forward and place them at an appropriate time."

Funeral practices are changing. Families seem to be finding help-ful ways to name the life of the one who has died. The family putting together a table of symbols or a photographic record of the life of the one who has died gives them an important voice at a time when words are difficult. Each family member, adults and children alike, might be encouraged to think of a symbol that depicts his or her re-lationship with the one who has died. The minister's role is to give people permission to bring the things that they might think are odd. Any symbol is an appropriate symbol and in the front of the church on a table beside the coffin it takes on a unique meaning. At the be-ginning or early in the service the family members might be encour-aged to bring the symbols forward and place them on a table at the front of the church. The movement allows a prayer that is physical and gives each family member a voice in the funeral service.

On the phone I mentioned asking to bring all the family together. You may need to remind the family of that offer and suggest a time. The family can then come together to remember the life of the one who has died. From that remembering they can plan the funeral service together. I would reiterate, "Remembering and naming the life of your (family member) is really important. I'd like to make a time when, with all the family who are available, we can sit and talk together when we can tell stories of what we remember of (use the name of the deceased). There will be all sorts of stories and memo-ries that it will be good to share. As you listen to each other you will identify some of the stories that you want to use in the service. You can ask, 'What are the stories that will tell the essence of this person's life?'" (Often they are the unexpected stories, the ones the family didn't think it would be appropriate to tell. They need permission and encouragement to use these stories, and as minister or theologi-cal interpreter you need to perceptively listen for and interpret these stories.)

Suggest to the family that one or more family members might like to use these or other stories to remember their family member (again, be sure to use that person's name). Initially family members are re-luctant and wonder if they will have the composure to do it. Encourage them by saying that even at the last minute, or even dur-ing the service, they can pull out if they want, and that if they have their material written out you will read it for them. Help them to un-derstand the importance of emotional expression at this time. "To cry in the service is appropriate. If you break down and cry it will give others permission to cry and, peculiarly, because you found it difficult to do, they will find it a more meaningful service."

There are other ways family members and friends can participate: choosing and playing appropriate music, singing, reading lessons or poems, and praying prayers. Giving permission and opening possibilities in encouraging ways will help people find voice at a really important time for them.

There is a peculiar growing trend that has people plan their own funeral before they die. They leave instructions written and unwritten about what is to happen in "my funeral." This is difficult. The funeral service is for those who are living, for the family and for the community. It provides for them an opportunity to acknowledge the life of the one who has died, and in their grief to touch those things that will give them consolation. So when a father says, "I want this hymn at my funeral," and this hymn seems inappropriate to the need for consolation of the family members, what happens? Or a mother says, "I don't want a funeral service," and the father is a person of faith who needs at this time to touch the resources of his faith; whose needs are most important at this time? I suspect that the trend to people planning their own funeral is a sign of the individualism of the present age and a fear that the living will not be able to acknowledge the life in an appropriate way. Death is a community experience and the community needs to be involved in acknowledging life and finding consolation. The faith community has thoughtfully planned liturgies in the light of the needs of the people and the promises of Christian faith.

I remember a special friend who was able to have a conversation with his dad about the funeral before his dad died. His dad said, "I have been from the church to the cemetery so many times I know my own way there. I don't want anybody to come to the cemetery," and nobody did. My friend found that very difficult. Whose rights are most important at this point? The funeral service is for the living and they ought to be able to touch and do the things that will be most appropriate for them at this time.

You can think of other things like this: Mary worships regularly, and her husband John has not been to church for years. Should Mary have John's funeral service in the church because it allows her to touch the things that will sustain her or should she have the funeral somewhere else because it reflects John's life? These are difficult questions to be addressed sensitively. We seek to offer that which heals, sustains, and gives life in the face of death.

Flowing from these conversations it should be possible to plan and enact appropriate funeral services. Significant, appropriate, and healing funeral services will emerge from such conversation.

The conversation doesn't end with the funeral service. Visiting after the funeral will enable an ongoing conversation to grow as grieving people come to terms with their changed life circumstance. It takes two years for people to recover from the grief of an expected death, more when the death is out of place.

"Winging It" in Pastoral Conversation

Olive

I went to the hospital to visit Olive. She was in her seventies, lived in subsidized housing near our church, and came to our senior citizens program for lunch each day. She was not part of our worshiping community. She had been admitted to hospital three weeks earlier. When I found out about her hospitalization I went to visit. Olive had no family. The only person who visited her was a man who long ago was engaged to her daughter, who had died.

In our conversation Olive mentioned how much she liked a mutual friend, Ethel. She said how friendly Ethel was and how easy it was for everyone to like her and to get along with her. I was thinking of another member of our community who was bitter about life, and rather intuitively said, "Not everyone gets on with her. I know one lady who can fight with her." Olive said, "Oh yes, she's a very bitter person."

Trying now to protect the person I had perhaps unwisely brought into the conversation, I said, "She's had a lot of pain in her life." Olive told me she had had a painful life too, and yet she had learned to live without becoming bitter. Here was an invitation to learn. I encouraged her to tell me about her life.

Tearfully at times, she told me the story of her life: that her parents separated when she was young and didn't want her; that she and her brother had been moved from place to place; that she had married a violent man and that she would walk the streets between 3 and 4 A.M., before beginning work at 7 A.M., because at home she would be beaten;

that she and her husband separated after she learned she could press charges against him for the violence; that when her daughter was nineteen, had a job, and was engaged to be married, one day she poured kerosene over her body and set herself alight. The daughter was hospitalized, needing skin grafts, which Olive donated. Her daughter died a month later—in the same hospital in which Olive was now a patient. All these memories had come flooding back. Later Olive learned that her former husband had hanged himself because "he had no one in life." She had indeed had a painful life.

Lying in her hospital bed, Olive was reviewing her life. She was not confident to name her faith and hope; certainly she was not confident to use religious language. Only a person who is in touch with God could come to terms with such experiences, make sense of them, and live a life of meaning and abundance. Part of my pastoral role is to be alert to and help people recognize and name their experiences. Then, I become an interpreter of the divine within that experience. In the midst of incredible tragedy and unanswerable questions, Olive had found a way to live her life without bitterness or fear and indeed with a sense of hope. I told Olive that I thought she must have been in touch with God to be able to live like that.

That is what it is to be in pastoral conversation. We are symbolic representatives of God who love the people given to our care. In loving, we use all that we can learn and know to listen and engage the living of the other. We seek to help people live their lives abundantly. We hope that their encounter with the Divine will be recognized and named, and that they will come to new and fresh speech.

In this book it has been my intention to stimulate your thinking about how you might engage pastoral conversation more confidently. I hope that in looking over my shoulder you will say, "I already do that," or, "I would like to try that." Building on the discipline and strategies suggested here I hope you will be encouraged to see your conversation as ministry, ministry enacted in the name of Jesus, giving form to the realm of God on earth.

I have wanted to name some things that might be helpful so that you might know what to do in those situations when you don't know what to do. I have suggested a basic discipline that will help you practice and become confident in some of the pastoral situations that you can anticipate. But every conversation will be different and drawing on all that you know, you will nonetheless occasionally have to "wing it."

Because I am an artist, drawing is basic to all that I do. Drawing is the discipline that undergirds and shapes how I make paintings. I practice drawing daily in order that I can take the discipline into my body. When I have the discipline then I can make marks with freedom, confidently knowing that they are formed from the discipline. There is a razor's edge between discipline and freedom. If I made free marks without the discipline of practicing drawing they would be boring and uninteresting scribble. Making free marks based on the discipline of drawing means that the marks come to life and will breathe and sing and dance in wonderful ways.

Conversation requires the same movement between the discipline of practicing and thinking about conversation and acting with freedom ("winging it") in particular conversations.

Treat every conversation that you enter as unique. Be present to the other, listen to each person as deeply as you possibly can. Seek to discern what someone wants from the conversation, then respond with the integrity of your own being as a person of faith. Whatever the situation, whatever the focus of the conversation, it will come to life and breathe and sing and dance in wonderful ways. You will be aware of the presence and image of God in the other person. You will be engaging deep and rich pastoral conversation. You will be giving body to God's realm in the world.

One last story

Susan's grandmother had been very important to her since both her parents had died when she was in her teens. When her grandmother died I went to visit.

Together with Susan's husband, Jeff, we talked about the funeral and whether the children should attend and how they would get on. I strongly advised them to take the children, saying that their children would take the funeral in their stride, and they would have a wisdom that will help adults cope with death. I suggested that when children share in funerals they learn something about life that enables them to develop into people who can live fully.

It wasn't just the death of Susan's grandmother that concerned Jeff and Susan at this time. Their eight-year-old daughter, Kylie, had her arm encased in plaster after an operation to remove part of the bone in her upper arm. On first look the doctor had thought it to be cancerous. That had raised the anxiety levels for this family.

Fortunately, the biopsy showed it was not. Kylie would have been alert to the anxiety in the family and the pain for her mum in the death of her grandmother. How do eight-year-olds get involved in conversations of such gravity? At the congregation's Christmas party two weeks later Kylie came to me three or four times during the afternoon and gave me some strong, affectionate cuddles and hugs. I sensed that this was a child's way of saying, "What you did when you came to talk with my Mum and Dad was very important, thanks." Of course, I am reading into her strong, physical response what I want to see. What else could I see? Families are systems and when I talked with Jeff and Susan in this family the children were also affected. Conversation reaches beyond those with whom you are immediately involved, and the response comes in ripples beyond our conscious knowing.

May God be with you and gift you as you seek to live Jesus' love in all your conversation.

BIBLIOGRAPHY

Anderson, Herbert, and Robert Cotton Fite. *Becoming Married*. Louisville: WJKP, 1993.

Anderson, Herbert, and Ed Foley. *Mighty Stories, Dangerous Rituals*. San Francisco: Jossey Bass, 1998.

Anderson, Herbert, David Hogue, and Marie McCarthy, SP. *Promising Again*. Louisville: WJKP, 1995.

Anderson, Herbert, and Kenneth Mitchell. *Leaving Home*. Louisville: WJKP, 1993.

Ashbrook, James B. *Minding the Soul.*, Minneapolis: Fortress, 1996.

Bass, Dorothy. *Practicing Our Faith*. San Francisco: Jossey Bass, 1999.

Cade, Brian, and William Hudson O'Hanlon. *A Brief Guide to Brief Therapy*. New York: W.W. Norton, 1993.

Carter, Betty, and Monica McGoldrick. *The Extended Family Life Cycle*. Boston: Allyn and Bacon, 1999.

Cowan, Michael A., and Bernard J. Lee. *Conversation Risk and Conversion*. Maryknoll, N.Y.: Orbis, 1997.

Faber, Heije, and Ebel van der Schoot, *The Art of Pastoral Conversation*. New York: Abingdon, 1965.

Fowler, James. *Stages of Faith*. Melbourne: Dove, 1981.

Friedman, Ed. *From Generation to Generation*. New York: Guildford, 1985.

Griffin, Graeme. *They Came to Care*. Melbourne: JBCE, 1993.

Haley, Jay. *Leaving Home*. New York: McGraw Hill, 1980.

Hunter, Rodney J. (ed.). *Dictionary of Pastoral Care and Counseling*. Nashville: Abingdon, 1990.

McGoldrick, Monica. *You Can Go Home Again*. New York: W.W. Norton, 1995/1997.

Mezirow, Jack, and Associates. *Learning as Transformation*. San Francisco: Jossey Bass, 2000.

Miller-McLemore, B., and B. L. Gill-Austern. *Feminist And Womanist Pastoral Theology*. Nashville: Abingdon, 1999.

Muller-Fahrenholz, Geiko. *The Art of Forgiveness*. Geneva, Switzerland: WCC, 1996/1997.

Palmer, Parker. *The Courage to Teach*. San Francisco: Jossey Bass 1998.

Patton, John, and Brian Childs. *Christian Marriage and Family*. Nashville: Abingdon, 1988.

Purnell, Douglas. *Exploring Your Family Story*. Melbourne: JBCE, 1983.

Wallerstein, Judith, and Sandra Blakeslee. *The Good Marriage*. London: Bantam Press, 1996.

Westberg, Granger E. *Good Grief*. Melbourne: JBCE, 1966.

Whitehead, E. E. and J. D. *Shadows of the Heart; A Spirituality of Negative Emotions*. New York: Crossroad, 1994.

Related titles available from The Pilgrim Press

CHALLENGING THE CHURCH MONSTER
From Conflict to Community

DOUGLAS J. BIXBY

ISBN 0-8298-1506-6/paper/128 pages/$16.00

The author's goal is to help pastors, as well as laity, to challenge the "church monster"—the personification of a wide variety of problems that have arisen in local churches as a result of the heightened levels of conflict and anxiety with which they are dealing. Accepting the challenge can bring fewer meetings, more ministry, and less conflict, and more community.

COMING OUT THROUGH FIRE
Surviving the Trauma of Homophobia

LEANNE MCCALL TIGERT AND TIMOTHY BROWN, EDS.

ISBN 0-8298-1293-8/paper/148 pages/$13.00

A book for lesbians, gays, bisexuals, and transgendered persons seeking to move through the trauma of homophobia with the passion and power of transformation. Also useful for pastors, therapists, and other counseling professionals who seek to confront prejudice and fear and further the process of healing and recovery in the church and the wider community.

DARING TO SPEAK IN GOD'S NAME
Ethical Prophecy in Ministry

MARY ALICE MULLIGAN AND RUFUS BURROW JR.

ISBN 0-8298-1492-2 / paper / 248 pages / $23.00

The coauthors challenge pastors to take on the role of the "ethical prophet"—one who dares to speak the truth in God's name in response to critical social issues of our day—and have created a model for ethical prophecy in today's times. Each chapter presents a discussion on practical applications for church settings and covers a wide variety of topics.

THE GENERATION-DRIVEN CHURCH
Evangelizing Boomers, Busters, and Millennials
WILLIAM BENKE AND LE ETTA BENKE

ISBN 0-8298-1509-0/paper/134 pages/$13.00

This book examines the cultural changes that have brought modern Christianity to where it is today. It defines characteristics of three generational categories—boomers, busters (generation X), and millennials (generation Y)—with related implications for ministry, providing some alternative strategies for helping inward-focused, small to mid-size churches take an expanded approach.

HOW TO GET ALONG WITH YOUR CHURCH
Creating Cultural Capital for Doing Ministry
GEORGE B. THOMPSON JR.

ISBN 0-8298-1437-X/paper/156 pages/$17.00

Thompson shares his observations and research as a pastor, emphasizing that in order for pastors to launch and maintain successful ministries, they must develop "cultural capital" within their congregations, that is, they must invest themselves deeply into how their church carries out its work and goes about its ministries.

INTRODUCING FEMINIST PASTORAL CARE AND COUNSELING
Introductions in Feminist Theology
NANCY J. GORSUCH

ISBN 0-8298-1440-X/paper/148 pages/$16.00

Another valuable resource in The Pilgrim Press's *Introductions in Feminist Theology* series. Feminist influence in pastoral care is both critical and constructive, and Gorsuch introduces feminist theology and psychotherapy as sources for caregivers, counselors, and others in ministry who want to draw from current revisions in theology and therapeutic theory.

THE LEADERSHIP OF JESUS AND ITS LEGACY TODAY
JOHN ADAIR

ISBN 0-8298-1510-4/paper/196 pages/$16.00

A captivating analysis of Jesus as a leader, then and now. Exploring the beliefs about leadership that were current in Jesus' day, Adair, a renowned author and consultant on leadership, sets out to discover what kind of leader Jesus was, comparing and contrasting his style with that of the secular and religious power-brokers of the time.

LEGAL GUIDE FOR DAY-TO-DAY CHURCH MATTERS
A Handbook for Pastors and Church Members, Revised and Expanded
CYNTHIA MAZUR AND RONALD BULLIS

ISBN 0-8298-1555-4/paper/160 pages/$10.00

This revised and expanded edition—compiled by attorney/ministers Mazur and Bullis—includes up-to-date legal materials for pastors and church members as well as information on the currently debated Faith-Based Initiative Program being supported by the Bush administration.

NOT WITHOUT A STRUGGLE
Leadership Development for African American Women in Ministry
VASHTI M. MCKENZIE

ISBN 0-8298-1076-5/paper/140 pages/$16.00

This groundbreaking book, written by one of America's leading African American clergywomen, provides a cogent historical, theological, and biblical overview of women's leadership in the church, in the hope of forging a new partnership among African American men and women.

PLENTY GOOD ROOM
Women Versus Male Power in the Black Church

MARCIA Y. RIGGS

ISBN 0-8298-1508-2 /paper/160 pages/$20.00

Riggs discusses African American church life as a case study for ethical reflection about sexual ethics and clergy ethics—the prevailing silence about sexuality in black churches and the fact that sexuality is generally a taboo in the Christian tradition—seeking to transform current discourse about sexual behavior and clergy misconduct from a concentration on formulating policy to retraining.

TROUBLE DON'T LAST ALWAYS
Emancipatory Hope Among African American Adolescents

EVELYN L. PARKER

ISBN 0-8298-1540-6 /paper/166 pages/$19.00

Parker critically examines African American adolescent spirituality and offers congregations a new theological framework for ministry with African American adolescents in the face of injustice and hopelessness. The intended result is the formulation of a wholesome spirituality.

YOUTH AT RISK
Ministry to the Least, the Lost, and the Last

PETER CHRISTIAN OLSEN

ISBN 0-8298-1556-2 /paper/128 pages/$14.00

Youth at Risk is a resource designed by Olsen, a youth minister and counselor, specifically for those who do ministry with at-risk youth. The book identifies basic developmental needs of at-risk youths, examines the derivation of these needs, and shows the Christian community how to respond to these needs.

To order these or any other books from The Pilgrim Press, call or write to:

THE PILGRIM PRESS
700 PROSPECT AVENUE
CLEVELAND, OH 44115-1100

Phone orders: 800-537-3394 (M–F, 8:30AM–4:30PM ET)
Fax orders: 216-736-2206

Please include shipping charges of $4.00 for the first book and 75¢ for each additional book.

Or order from our Web site at www.pilgrimpress.com.

Prices subject to change without notice.